Yamuna's Journey

Baba Padmanji

Translated from the Marathi by
Deepra Dandekar

SPEAKING TIGER BOOKS LLP
125A, Ground Floor, Shahpur Jat, near Asiad Village,
New Delhi 110049

First published by Speaking Tiger Books 2022

Copyright © Baba Padmanji 2022
Translation copyright © Deepra Dandekar 2022

ISBN: 978-93-5447-361-6
eISBN: 978-93-5447-359-3

10 9 8 7 6 5 4 3 2 1

All rights reserved.
No part of this publication may be reproduced, transmitted,
or stored in a retrieval system, in any form or by any means,
electronic, mechanical, photocopying, recording or otherwise,
without the prior permission of the publisher.

This book is sold subject to the condition that it shall not,
by way of trade or otherwise, be lent, resold, hired out,
or otherwise circulated, without the publisher's prior
consent, in any form of binding or cover other
than that in which it is published.

Baba Padmanji Mulay was born in 1831 in Belgaum. A firebrand pioneer of Christian feminist reform in 19th-century Western India, Padmanji hailed from an elite, conservative family that was non-Brahmin in terms of caste—the *tvashta kasar* caste of braziers. He converted to Christianity in 1854 and thereafter came into conflict with various intellectual Hindu reform groups in Bombay such as the Paramhans Mandali and the Prarthana Samaj and its associates. Padmanji married multiple times after divorcing his first Hindu wife in 1857, which had a lasting impact on him. The author of over a hundred Marathi texts, he ran his own printing press (Victoria Press) in Bombay. Serving as an ordained pastor at the Free Church in Pune for some time after 1861, Padmanji retired as the head of the Bombay Vernacular Books Society, and as editor of numerous Christian journals from Western India. He passed away in August 1906 in Mumbai and lies buried at the Sewri Christian Cemetery.

Deepra Dandekar is a researcher at the Leibniz-Zentrum Moderner Orient, Berlin. She is the author of *Baba Padmanji: Vernacular Christianity in Colonial India,* the first critical biography of Baba Padmanji in English. She can be contacted at Deepra.Dandekar@zmo.de

Translator's Dedication

For my mother

Contents

Note for Readers ix
Translator's Introduction xiii

1. Marriage 1
2. Khandu the Barber 8
3. Venu's Story 14
4. The Imposter's Disguise 29
5. The Wig 39
6. The Maidservant's Trickery 48
7. Cheated! 56
8. Those Reformed 64
9. Released 69
10. The Brahmin Widow 74
11. The Conference 91
12. Arjun and the Lady 107
13. The Moment of Decision 115

14. Death	122
15. The Gathering of Clouds	135
16. The Final Twist	146
17. The Test	153
18. Shivram	162
Glossary	177

Note for Readers

When Baba Padmanji (1831-1906) wrote *Yamunaparyatan* in 1857—the first vernacular novel in India—he also meant to provide a realistic account of the travails suffered by Hindu widows in Bombay Presidency, and India in general, based on empirical facts. However, to make the book more accessible to Marathi readers, Padmanji composed these empirical facts in a novelized format that located *Yamunaparyatan* as a literary enterprise, situated between the realistic and the fictional. This dilemma of 'in-between-ness' for the evolving vernacular genres of the 19th century, continued well into the 20th and 21st centuries, evidenced within translations. Though I have kept Padmanji's arguments intact, I have at other places paraphrased, and desisted from providing verbatim translations, especially when Padmanji quotes Sanskrit passages or older Marathi religious texts. Since these verbatim translations do not add special meaning to the storyline, I have simplified the text in places, though I have also striven not to render it too simplistic.

Focusing only on Yamuna's story in this translation would have defeated Padmanji's purpose of placing *Yamunaparyatan* within larger debates surrounding widow-remarriage in the years 1856 and 1857. Therefore, I have added a descriptive introduction that provides readers with further historical information on the novel's context. However, this is also a story meant to be enjoyed, and so, in keeping with Padmanji's aim of writing a fledgling romantic novel, I have desisted from making the text too academic. I have not used diacritical marks and nor have I provided any footnotes. Instead, retaining certain vernacular terms to give the reader a feel for the novel's original flavour, I have provided a glossary in the end that explains the meaning of these vernacular words in context. Since the original *Yamunaparyatan* contains voluminous introductions, prefaces, and appendices, written in some instances in Sanskrit by Padmanji's close associate Dadoba Pandurang—a public figure centrally linked to the Prarthana Samaj in Bombay—I have left these out and described some of its contents in the translator's introduction as well.

There are many friends, whom I must thank for this book, beginning with librarians of the British Library in London, who provided me with the original 1857 edition of *Yamunaparyatan*. I also thank all those who assisted me in writing the first critical biography of Baba Padmanji in English, *Baba Padmanji: Vernacular Christianity in Colonial India* published in 2021 by the Routledge Pathfinders series. It is from that critical biography that this English translation of *Yamunaparyatan* has emerged, and I thank my readers, especially Naresh Fernandes, for their encouragement. I am grateful to the editors at Speaking Tiger Books for showing this book the light of day, nearly a century-and-a-half after it was first published in Marathi.

—Deepra Dandekar

Translator's Introduction

Yamunaparyatan (*Yamuna's Journey*) is a title with multiple messages. While the title connotes a holy pilgrimage, a journey to the River Yamuna, one of the most sacred rivers of India, the name also harks to a tradition that has Vrindavan, that flanks the River Yamuna, witness millions of destitute Hindu widows arriving every year, a practice of the last few hundred years or more. These widows spend their old age in a pathetic condition on the banks of the Yamuna, abandoned by their families, and reviled as orphans.

They beg for food, have no access to medical care, and ultimately waste away into a sad and lonely death. Considered to only be the wives of Lord Krishna, it is unnecessary to underline how exploited widows, especially the young and orphaned, are. *Yamunaparyatan* also describes the physical journey that was poignantly experienced by the novel's protagonist, a young lady called Yamuna, who travels across various regions of the Bombay Presidency and Western India. Yamuna's journey is central to the story, as her interaction with many widows during this journey reveals the extent of their torture and humiliation within Hindu patriarchal and Brahminical society. *Yamunaparyatan*, in addition, connotes Yamuna's spiritual journey towards education and the realization of God that is similar to the meaning of pilgrimage discussed above, but for the fact that Yamuna ultimately converts to Christianity in the novel.

The journey of Yamuna is hence a metaphor used by Baba Padmanji to identify a widow's journey towards salvation, and to Christianity as its only meaningful spiritual source available for exploited and tortured Hindu widows. Conversion, he indicated, would help especially upper-caste widows, whose families forced them to endure tonsure and many other privations and indignities, to choose widow-remarriage as a decent, moral path that would help resettle their lives. Finally, *Yamunaparyatan* is also about Yamuna's marital relationships. Yamuna starts off as a youthful married woman in the beginning of the novel, very much in love with her husband, and then proceeds almost inexorably towards widowhood. Tortured as a widow, she converts to Christianity in the end and remarries a young Christian man. The title *Yamunaparyatan* is hence, layered, and Padmanji uses it to describe the only possible solution to the humiliation of enforced widowhood—remarriage, with or without conversion, but of course, preferably with conversion.

Since familial abandonment and the abject poverty and neglect of widows still remains an unresolved issue for Hindus, as widows continue to languish in pilgrimage towns like Vrindavan (Uttar Pradesh) or Phaltan (Maharashtra), this makes the English translation of *Yamunaparyatan* relevant and timely for many Indian feminists today—a creative thought experiment from the 19th century about what continues to be a problem. The tragedy of Hindu widows and the afterlife of their remarriage in terms of the anxiety it historically produced, regenerates itself within Hindu-Brahminical society in a way that cannot be summarily dismissed as limited to the mentality of an uneducated few. Well-known writer Girish Karnad's autobiography *This Life at Play: Memoirs* (HarperCollins, 2021) dwells poignantly and in significant detail on his childhood trauma due to the gossip about his mother's morality. She was a widow with a young child when she married his father. The travails of Hindu widowhood and the anxiety about widow-remarriage are hence interlinked.

In Padmanji's eyes, this needless anxiety required eradication, and that could not be achieved without breaking from the tensions of Hinduism itself.

Within Hinduism, the anxiety about the widow's sexual morality and remarriage would only continue to perpetuate the stigma of widowhood. Widow-remarriage within the public imagination would, hence, never be entirely free of indignity, stigma, and anxiety for women. Padmanji fiercely attacked this very stigma and anxiety when addressing it in *Yamunaparyatan*, and promoted religious conversion for widows that would not only enable remarriage, but would also eradicate the stigma of widowhood—something also advocated by Pandita Ramabai when seeking a break with the impurity and inauspiciousness ascribed to widows within Hinduism.

Padmanji converted to Christianity in 1854 and was a fresh convert in 1856 when he wrote *Yamunaparyatan* (published a year later). He was extremely zealous, his enthusiasm more than evident in the passion with which he wrote between the years 1851 and 1860. However, the years preceding and immediately after his conversion were not easy, especially since 1857 also marked the year of his divorce from his first Hindu wife, who instigated by her family because of his own conversion to Christianity, left him. Perhaps, it was because of this personal, rather poignant ecology of the book, that Padmanji imagined and portrayed Yamuna's personality in *Yamunaparyatan* as a paragon of rational and Protestant, Christian reformist values.

At other times, she was also his alter ego, converting to Christianity and remarrying just as Padmanji himself did, four years after his divorce.

The year 1856 was also a turbulent one in the history of widow-remarriage debates and discussions in India, for it was in 1856 that Ishwar Chandra Vidyasagar, after arguing for widow-remarriage on the basis of Sanskrit scriptures, caused quite a stir among Brahmins by getting the widow-remarriage bill passed in the British-Indian Parliament. The social ecology of *Yamunaparyatan* therefore, also powerfully consisted of the widow-remarriage act and Vidyasagar's advocacy of it. Padmanji strongly championed Vidyasagar, and much of the novel's storyline that contains debates between intellectuals on the subject, follow the widow-remarriage arguments that were presented by Vidyasagar. The two appendices of the novel provide readers not only with the text of the widow-remarriage act but also a short background description of Vidyasagar's activism, and a description of the first widow-remarriages that took place in Bengal. Though 1857 stands out in Indian historiography as the year of a large uprising against the East India Company, the same year also stands out as the direct aftermath of the widow-remarriage act.

Some rumblings in the direction of religious sentiments associated with the 1857 uprising can already be glimpsed from certain passages of *Yamunaparyatan*, though Padmanji (writing these chapters in 1856), could hardly have predicted the uprising. The chapters outlining discussions about widow-remarriage among Hindu Brahmin scholars articulate their anger and dissatisfaction with the British, as they justified widowhood practices as indigenous to Hinduism, that were moreover perceived as a device of anti-colonial resistance. The British were accused in these debates of interfering with religion, ancient Hindu traditions, and community sentiments by first banning Sati and then widowhood practices. Conversion, reform, and modernity were criticized in these chapters as successful British measures that sought to weaken Hindu anti-colonial resistance.

Although Padmanji remained uncritical of the British, and even openly praised missions in chapter 18, the book graphically reveals the extent of British interference in the reproductive lives of women—especially widows (chapter 12). Padmanji was critical of Hindu customary values that harmed women, considering them to be sedimented aspects of society that were justified as anti-colonial resistance, and thereby non-reflexively reified as an essentialist part of Hindu identity, predicated on Brahminism. At the same time, he was a staunch Christian convert with robust and passionate Protestant values, who considered it correct of the government to criminalize the abortion and killing of infants, especially feticide.

As it comes across in many parts of the novel, such as in chapters 4 and 13, Padmanji likened Hindus to Roman Catholics and ascribed the debasement of their religion to cultures of courtly decadence. It was not Hinduism per se that Padmanji criticized, though he did consider it too archaic and obscure as a modern, moral guide for adherents in a changing world defined by science and cosmopolitanism. In the same vein, he pointed out how customary Hinduism was severely detrimental to Hindus, and to Indian society at large.

The story of *Yamunaparyatan* is layered but straightforward, describing the travails of widows, whom the protagonist Yamuna meets during her journey. These accounts are accompanied by descriptions of their opinion about religion, morality, and caste; marriage, family, and female sexuality; and reform, conversion, and colonialism. Perhaps predictably, *Yamunaparyatan* received tremendous criticism after it was published. Hindus accused the book of encompassing a subterfuge, beginning with a Sanskrit passage that masqueraded as a Hindu text, and which distracted readers from what these critics saw as the novel's original intent: justifying conversion, depleting Brahminical bulwark by converting away women and widows, and indirectly missionizing.

Padmanji was accused of peddling conversion under the garb of Hindu reform, despite the book's vociferous critique of Hindu reformers (chapter 8). The book has a lengthy preface written by Dadoba Pandurang that contains an overview of Sanskrit verses in support of widow-remarriage, and Padmanji provides a Marathi paraphrase of it, in addition to his own *prastavana* (introduction) that exhorts young men to marry widows, endorsing action rather than verbal discussion. Padmanji uses the metaphor of a time traveller to describe the incomplete and hesitant nature of Hindu reform, wondering what a time traveller from the past, visiting the modern future of 1857 would find, when investigating the position of women in Indian society. This time traveller, Padmanji lamented, would only discover the modern woman as fragmented and a shattered entity, her identity entrapped within archaic traditional shards from an obscure past that shackled her, even as it tried to simultaneously free her. Depicting contradictions and paradoxes inherent to this imagined fragmented, traditional-modern woman of 1857, Padmanji's language remained quite graphic (p. 7):

'Her face is fair, and her hands are beautiful. But her feet are dark and ugly, filled with the marks of skin disease. Her clothes are a patchwork of different kinds of cloth stitched together. While some of these are exquisite silk brocade, many are stained with dirt and patched over with cheap rags. Many are old and frayed, their edges plain or embroidered with silk. If her ornaments be described, many are ornate and beautiful. She has a pearl necklace around her neck, but if closely inspected, many pearls are broken and replaced in places by cowrie shells. Her wrists are adorned with expensive, heavy gold bangles, but accompanied by bracelets of tin. Her ankles are adorned with heavy silver anklets, but so tightly bound by iron chains that she cannot take a step forward. Since her face is beautiful, she only says nice things. She may buy fresh foods and delicacies from the market, but keeps them for many days first, to ensure that they grow stale and rot. Only thereafter does she eat them, or does not eat at all despite having food, ensuring that she falls ill from fasting. Likewise, her house is strewn with expensive things that are uncared for and lying abandoned.'

Yamunaparyatan was also criticised for the rather rough and ribald language that Padmanji used to describe women's sexual relationships outside marriage, their pregnancies, and home abortions. Padmanji's detractors claimed that his language was so foul that the book did not deserve the status of the first vernacular novel; and that it would only bring shame to Marathi literature. Padmanji, on the other hand, claimed that his novel was based on empirical research, and its main storyline was composed of empirical anecdotes about the difficulties Hindu widows faced in patriarchal Brahminical society. It was never meant to be a poetic, aesthetic book, and was always meant to be hard hitting, and a realistic treatise. Empirical anecdotes in this case were woven together into a single narrative, and only written in the form of a novel.

Other literary critics of the postcolonial period blamed this anecdotal nature of *Yamunaparyatan* as responsible for the book falling short of a full-blown novel, and more akin to the traditional *kadambari* genre consisting of interwoven stories. It was mostly ignored that the story-within-a-story format was deliberately chosen by Padmanji to compose his empirical research into a fictionalized narrative. It was not as if he had set out to write a modern novel, but, unable to achieve this goal, had ended up falling short of it and written a *kadambari* instead. Well-versed in the genre of novels (especially in English), he never attempted to ever write a *kadambari* in the first place. Though *Yamunaparyatan* was composed as a novel, its various painstakingly collected anecdotes were presented as empirical facts, evident in chapter 3, and explicitly mentioned in chapter 12. These anecdotes were based on eyewitness reports, describing how the Hindu-Brahminical marriage system exploited and tortured women, first, by not educating them and then, by treating them unequally, and accusing them of foolishness and for being inauspicious—'the source of all sorrows'.

To quote some of his own opinions about the novel that he refers to simply as 'book' or *pustak* in his *prastavana*, Padmanji views *Yamunaparyatan* as a collective enterprise based on empirical research, concerning contemporary debates on widow-remarriage. This collective nature can be gleaned from Padmanji's acknowledgement of all those who sent him empirical case studies about widowhood, as stated in his *prastavana* (p. 12):

'Now in the end, I thank all my educated and reformed friends who helped me write this book by sending me urgent reports and descriptions about widowhood from many places in South Maharashtra. I am especially grateful to Dadoba Pandurang, who has paid close attention to this subject and helped me tremendously. The essay in Sanskrit that is added to the beginning of the book has been written by him, and will be doubtless of great interest to many renowned textual scholars. In fact, it would have been wonderful, and even more useful, if one of them, or scholars as great as them, had come forward to write a book on this subject.'

Deeply influenced by Rev. Surendra Nath Banerjea and his writings on women's education and emancipation, Padmanji described the piteous situation of those young girls, who were married off hastily as children to men decades older than themselves. Not only were they subjected to sexual abuse within such alliances, but also subjected to domestic abuse in the household, worked hard by the older women of the family. Squeezed between marital duties, childbirth, and heavy domestic work, young girls became victims of their marital families. After their husbands died, they were subjected to further torture—tonsure, inadequate food and clothing, ill-treatment, a heavier than ever workload, and no creature comforts whatsoever. Padmanji argued that women within Brahminical families were constantly on the brink of abandonment and destitution, suffering deeply from the fear of becoming outcasts, even before they became widows.

To become widowed was their greatest worry and anxiety that was central to their lives as upper-caste women. Reviled once they became widowed, many young women finally either committed suicide (chapter 2) or ran away from home (chapter 4) and turned to prostitution (chapters 6 and 12). This situation of gendered helplessness may have altered since the 19th century, but it has not transformed too fundamentally for single women in the sense of the systemic violence they continue to suffer. Padmanji's criticism of Hindu religious texts like the *Gurucharitra* (chapter 15) and the *Dasbodh* (chapter 10), hence, require to be understood within the context of reform. Padmanji's criticism was not simply an expression of empty polemics, but served an important purpose of demonstrating how the emulation of scriptures could no longer serve the purpose of a reformed society necessary for the equality between men and women. Padmanji was similarly critical of many dictums contained in Hindu scriptures that blamed wives for their husbands' deaths, and blamed widows for jeopardizing their husbands' afterlives, by refusing to tonsure their heads. In fact, descriptions of widowhood rituals provided in chapters 7, 10, 16, and 17 clearly demonstrate how widowhood rituals actually subverted the sati abolishment act of 1829 and continued perpetuating the values of sati.

Padmanji was a staunch and pioneering feminist. He believed women to be equal to men. He believed that women and men were to be educated exactly alike, and given equal access to professional opportunities. He considered spouses as equal marital and romantic partners marked by a special friendship, and did not believe in the subservience of wives to husbands. He wanted both men and women to choose their spouses after attaining adulthood—an individual and personal choice predicated on intellectual friendship and attraction, irrespective of caste, and outside the purview of family arrangements. He believed that widows should be as independent as widowers, and supported widow-remarriage, while further endorsing the property and inheritance rights of widows.

He was fiercely critical of the stigma accorded to widows within Brahminical-Hinduism and fought it tooth and nail. In fact, the most enduring legacy of *Yamunaparyatan* is its portrayal of equal, romantic, conjugal partnerships, depicted between spouses of the same age, who shared religious, intellectual, emotional, and moral proclivities and insights; spouses who were constantly in conversation and discussion with each other. Yamuna was not her husband's junior, and their relationship constituted an ideal example of conjugal marital relationships for young, reformed, educated, and modern readers, who could emulate the model—a decent, yet pleasurable paradigm of marital love that held equality between spouses as a core value. *Yamunaparyatan* is hence, a surprisingly modern book that can be considered the forerunner of later-day postcolonial, feminist literature that also explores relationships between genders within Marathi society.

One of Padmanji's greatest anxieties was concerned with the hesitation of the educated and the reformed youth in taking the step to remarry widows. Without this action, their education, Padmanji felt, was wasted. This is a concern he strongly highlights in the last chapter of *Yamunaparyatan*, when one of the book's junior protagonists outlines an evolved idea of running an organized, crowd funded, social movement in favour of widow remarriage. Expressing this frustration through a metaphor of salt and seawater—a metaphor that Gandhi himself, perhaps coincidentally later adopted in 1930 to show the 'action-oriented' nature of Indian independence from the British—Padmanji says in his *prastavana*

(pp. 9-10):

'Even if seawater is filled with salt, it is inadequate to know this. Salt has to be intentionally removed from the seawater with specific, scientific actions. Similarly, thoughts of widow-remarriage that have penetrated the minds of our reformed, educated youth, like salt in seawater, need to be mindfully extracted and transformed into thoughtful, well-intended action that will not only first separate that salt but also enable its use.'

Though he was a staunch feminist, Padmanji's feminism did have its limits. He was a great believer in the institution of marriage for women, and *Yamunaparyatan* was therefore, also transformed into a space where he articulated the promise of happiness, that reformed marriages held out for couples who could live together with social awareness, even if one of them became widowed. Just like his critical approach to customary Brahminism, Padmanji strongly opposed courtly culture, especially the strong culture of public entertainment in the Deccan that involved musical soirees and dances performed by courtesans. Many traditional courtesans and prostitutes in *Yamunaparyatan* spoke a mixed variety of Urdu and Marathi (referring, for example, to young girls in their service as *bachcha*) that belied their roots within courtly culture.

Padmanji was additionally opposed to the percolation of courtly culture among rural, landed elites, in the form of *tamasha*, patronized by Brahmins, and other upper castes, that similarly involved musical performances by courtesans whose profession bordered on outright prostitution, as is evident in chapter 11. Padmanji, hence, fixed the limits of his tolerance, despite sympathy for widows, at sexual relationships, pregnancies, and childbirth outside marriage, though he identified these as either the result of the unfair exploitation of women, or the products of courtly, cultural, and social decadence. His Protestant rage is clearly reflected in the harsh words he uses for women engaged in such sexual alliances.

Padmanji was also a staunch supporter of the Protestant missions of India as institutional spaces that fostered freedom, education, philosophy, equality, learning, and morality—a gift from the British missions to India. He strongly felt that British missions helped Indians in expanding their social vista, reflected in the discussions of chapters 11 and 18. He extolled a new variety of ecology emerging from missionary life that had resulted in rational town-planning, free, sanitized, and clean spaces, and clean air that avoided clustering too close together. In many parts of *Yamunaparyatan*, Padmanji praises the mission and its education system, reiterating the need for Indians to respond to this education by reforming their society through institutional measures modelled on the mission.

He praised missionary villages and inhabitations as new, modern areas of cleanliness, hygiene, governance, and good health that fostered individual growth and a rational avoidance of epidemics. A question that has often been asked—a question based on the assumption that religious life and social life are, and were, essentially and always different—is whether Padmanji's feminism was really feminist at all, or was it just general Protestantism? To answer that question with a quote from *Yamunaparyatan*'s introduction (page 11), Protestantism and feminism were hardly different for Padmanji. He writes:

'Many will dislike the opinions that the protagonists Yamuna-bai and Vinayak-rao have expressed in this book, with some even saying that there is no connection between widow-remarriage and such opinions. Perhaps they would even be right, if we were to accept that women, like the Chinese say, do not possess eternal souls. Or then, if we consider women to be like animals and write books about them with titles like 'The Mare of the Ghorpades', or 'Ramji Patil's Gentle Bull', or 'Godavari-bai's Kashi Cow', or 'The Bhavani Goat of Dhangar Malhari', or 'The Malahan Buffalo of Krishna Milkman', or 'The Mani Cat of Putala-bai', or for that matter 'The Brave Monkey'. In these stories we do not need to worry about the souls of the animals described. But if women have eternal souls, then it is important to think of their present condition and future. This book is as concerned about the happiness of "this world" that the women and widows of our country and society deserve, as I am of the happiness of their "other world". They must be free from the life of physical and mental slavery, reach positions of esteem and honour that match their capacity, and redeem their eternal soul of all sins to achieve even greater honour in heaven.'

Another question that is often asked, modelled on the first is: was Padmanji a reformist or a missionary? Again, these two were not separate identities for Padmanji, as he considered conversion itself to constitute an act of reforming. Often reiterating the difficulties of reforms internal to Hinduism, and the superficiality of Hindu reformers in *Yamunaparyatan* that left widows in the lurch, and the fact that widow remarriage within Hinduism hardly addressed the anxiety about the sexual morality of widows—as evident from the case of Girish Karnad and his mother—converting to Christianity for Padmanji, was the only solution and the only true reform that would bring about a change in women's conditions, and eradicate their torture and humiliation within Brahminical-Hinduism.

Finally, Padmanji was making a demographic point in *Yamunaparyatan*, of how Hindus were reducing the number of women in their own society through female infanticide (chapter 11) or widowhood practices that placed an increasing number of women outside the socially and morally accepted reproductive fold. If Hindu society was bent on self-destruction by eliminating its women, then Padmanji felt that they had no right to be offended if these same women converted and lived respectful lives thereafter, as part of the Christian community that accorded them equality and dignity.

Resonating in his opinion with later-day feminists, he emphasized that women treated as educated adults, capable of making their own life decisions, marry whomever they wanted, or remarry, constituted an asset for the Indian family, society, and country. Their capable presence and action would only help families, children, and men, and assist in producing a society and country that was equal, healthy, and a moral place for everyone. Not focusing particularly on the plight of lower-caste Hindus, Padmanji instead criticized middle-caste Hindus (like the goldsmith caste, or Prabhus) for ritually allying with Brahmins. The solution for him thus lay, not in focusing on lower-caste emancipation, but in strongly divesting Brahmins and Brahminism of demographic support, singling them out, and subjecting them to legal measures, social activism, and compulsory re-education.

What makes *Yamunaparyatan* special is its bold feminist ideas expressed in a very early period—much before Christian feminism in the UK. Reading this novel more than a hundred and fifty years after it was first published, one still feels the currency of the feminist issues that Padmanji raised.

Rev. Baba Padmanji Mulay
(image from his autobiography published in 1892, Madras,
Basel University Library: Thl Cv 583:10)

1

Marriage

The April heat of the *Vaishakh* month is usually stifling. Ganesh-*pant*, covered in a cooling unguent of fine sandalwood paste, sat musingly on a large swing seat in his front room, hoping for some cool breeze. Just as he was beginning to feel a trifle calm, Vithal-*bhatji*, the family astrologer came by with a message from Raghoba-*pant*.

Ganesh-*pant*: 'Come in. Come in. Has our plan succeeded?'

Vithal-*bhatji*: 'It must succeed when I mediate, after all! Now, do I finally get the *dhoti*s you promised?'

Ganesh-pant: 'Don't you worry! You will have the best *dhoti*s in the world. Once the occasion goes according to plan, I will present you with the best chintz *dhoti*s that were ever made in Nagpur and sold at Khushal-*shet*'s shop.'

Vithhal-*bhatji*: 'Well, Raghoba-*pant* can hardly wait to settle the date.'

Ganesh-*pant*: 'Forget the formalities and decide quickly on the first available date. All the preparations are complete from my side, and if you don't believe me, go upstairs, and see for yourself. Vinayak is sitting in the attic, making a list of expenses. Also, ask him what happened about exchanging your wife's *sarees* at Ghan-*shet*'s shop.'

Vithhal-*bhatji*, once upstairs: 'How are things, dear bridegroom? How is your bride's jewellery coming along? Is her necklace grand enough? I know she wanted that ornate one. Be careful not to anger your new bride! I must compliment you both for making such a handsome couple. She suits you perfectly.'

Vinayak sat quietly, blushing as Vithhal-*bhatji* left, bidding Ganesh-*pant* a hasty farewell.

The wedding date was fixed for the first day of *Jyeshtha*, and from that time onwards, Yamuna began visiting her in-laws regularly. Gifts of mangoes, jackfruit, and sweetmeats began arriving, and her mother-in-law grew very fond of her. She would dress Yamuna in finery and jewels, and comb her hair in various styles, decorating her braid with flowers and ornaments. She would flaunt Yamuna to her friends and relatives, and everyone would pamper Yamuna, offering her candy, fruits, and gifts of pretty brocade blouses. Vinayak, the prospective bridegroom, was jubilant too, regaling his friends with Yamuna's talents.

His friends would praise Yamuna, saying, 'Vinayak, your wife's handwriting is as beautiful as printed letters! What intelligence! Not only is her arithmetic perfect, but her embroidery is divine too.'

Vinayak would internally glow hearing all this.

Yamuna was not just beautiful and talented, but also educated. However, it was precisely her education that her mother-in-law disliked the most about Yamuna. Yamuna's father, Raghoba-*pant*, had been poor, and had therefore sent her to a missionary school, where she had received money, food, and clothes in exchange for attending school. This education had polished Yamuna's natural intelligence and honed her capacity for independent thought. In terms of confidence, her educated intelligence made her superior to other girls around her. Sadly, however, apart from her husband, no one really appreciated Yamuna. It was Yamuna's mother, before passing away, who had requested Ganesh-*pant* to accept Yamuna as a daughter-in-law for his beloved son Vinu. Ganesh-*pant*, in his gentlemanly way, had kept his promise, and proceeded with the marriage.

Yamuna and Vinayak got married in great pomp. Though her father was poor, he had amassed enough money to give an impression of a financial status deemed suitable for his friend Ganesh-*pant*. After the first days of festivities, however, everyone forgot how much money had been wasted, and life went on as usual. In the first days after marriage, Yamuna would sometimes stay with her father. She was not allowed to read and write when staying with her in-laws, and her time there would pass in dressing up, visiting relatives, and participating in ritual celebrations. She would make wicks for the household temple's oil lamps, help in cooking and cleaning, and generally, while away her time feeling bored. There was no opportunity to read or learn anything new, as her mother-in-law and sister-in-law refused to leave her alone, or let her read. Moreover, the topics they discussed were puerile and petty. Staying constantly in their company gradually whittled away at Yamuna's own intelligence, and stemmed her natural curiosity—a desire imbibed at school. Now, her mind was filled with anxieties, superstitions, and foolish falsehoods.

One afternoon, as she sat cleaning rice grains, her mother-in-law, and sister-in-law—Ganga, joined her, and they began a conversation.

Mother-in-law: 'Ganga, why did you not finish the *poli* from yesterday? You girls don't eat properly at home, and then act greedy at other people's homes. Yamuna, did you give the servant boy the remaining rice? And oh, why did you tell him about the remaining *poli*? I had told you to give him only the rice.'

Yamuna, in a low voice: 'Yes, but he asked me directly for *poli*. How could I have lied?'

Mother-in-law: 'Oh God, what a goldmine of truth we have here! A girl must never think for herself. Instead, she must always do as she is told.'

Ganga: 'Yes, mother, I, too, have noticed this! The other day, when a visitor came, she went and told him that father was sleeping, even though he had explicitly instructed us to tell visitors that he was out.'

Yamuna: 'So what? At least I didn't lie.'

Ganga: 'This is what happens when girls are sent to school by their ignorant parents!'

Mother-in-law: 'Stop it, you girls! But yes, Yamuna's education cannot continue. She will have to accept the discipline of this house. Didn't you see what happened next door to Ramji-*pant*'s sister? She mended her ways alright and now demurely circles the family *tulsi* a hundred and eight times every day. Her sister-in-law sold all her books to a wastepaper vendor. Yamuna will do so too.'

Yamuna's heart quailed. Who knew her learning would come to an end so soon? These women would never let her read ever again!

Her mother-in-law, indifferent to the turmoil in Yamuna's heart, continued: 'Girls! Before going out for the picnic tomorrow, I want you to eat curd rice at home so that you don't feel too hungry till lunchtime.'

Yamuna decided to elicit her husband's help. She devised ways to meet and talk to him in private, and soon, the husband and wife became friends. Yamuna began confiding her secrets in Vinayak, and told him about his mother's and sister's taunts. Vinayak, not being thoughtless and selfish like other boys, listened carefully and patiently. He tried to comfort Yamuna, and gave her more freedom in the time they spent together. She could do as she liked when she was with him. Thereafter, she often escaped to their room in her spare time, and sat there reading books. It filled her with happiness. This is how the young couple fell in love. They trusted each other and tried to resolve their difficulties together, making enlightened, educated, and mature decisions. Yamuna was a soft-hearted and sensitive girl. She would tremble, sweat, and worry, and feel cornered very easily, feeling upset at the slightest hint of being forced into anything against her will. As household responsibilities and the expectations of her increased, Yamuna became thin with worry and fear of her mother-in-law and sister-in-law.

Noticing her deteriorating health, Vinayak asked affectionately one day: 'Why do you grow thinner by the day, my dear? Is something worrying you?'

Yamuna: 'I am plagued with so much anxiety that I no longer care for physical comforts and pleasures. I feel eternally burdened by an emotional turmoil.'

Vinayak: 'Do tell me your worries! I love you so much that I can give my life for you.'

Yamuna: 'I am grateful that God has given you to me as a husband. Though we are on earth for a short time, I hope we will be together in the next world ever after.'

Vinayak's eyes filled with tears. Wiping his eyes with a kerchief, he assured Yamuna: 'Please don't talk of death my dear. With God's blessings, you will soon feel better with medicines.'

2

Khandu the Barber

Vinayak and Yamuna were standing in their garden admiring the beautiful sunset. As Vinayak held up a jasmine flower for Yamuna's inspection, commenting on God's ingenious glory that created such a beautiful flower, they were startled by sudden screams emanating from next doors. As he ran there, Vinayak heard a heavy splash in the backyard. Not paying much heed to the splash, he ran to the neighbour's back door. Finding a man standing there silently reading a letter, surrounded by four or five wailing women, Vinayak enquired what had happened. The man silently handed him the letter.

It read:

It grieves me to announce that Shivram Gopal has passed away today. He had high fever this last week, and failed to respond to medical treatment. However, though he was a good person, he had recently become corrupted by reformist ideas. He had begun supporting widow-remarriage, and opposed Hindu customs about the tonsuring of widows. It was finally his arrogance that led to a fall! I suggest you tonsure his widow immediately. Remove her bangles, finery, sell off her ornaments, and give her coarse cloth to wear. She must not henceforth sleep on a bed, and must only use a couple of blankets on the floor. Make haste! The girl's brother is equally corrupted by reformist ideas, and if he gets wind of her widowhood, he is likely to whisk her away before the ritual. Her tonsuring should commence forthwith.

Vinayak was overcome with shock, his heart filling with poignant rage and grief. But he felt helpless. He could not intervene with the family matters of outsiders, even if they were neighbours. He asked who had sent the letter, and he also asked solicitously about Shivram's wife. The letter, he was told, had been written by Shivram's uncle, and also, that no one knew or cared where Shivram's wife was hiding at present. When Vinayak firmly asked the loitering children to find her, one of the ladies at the back door remarked acerbically: 'Why do you look for her now? The most important person is gone! What does the family have to do with her now—an inauspicious creature in essence. First, her brother-in-law died, followed by her mother-in-law. Then her father died, and now she has killed her own husband. She is a burden for this family now, weighing on us like a stone.'

Another lady remarked: 'She is the very personification of bad luck. The whore has destroyed the entire family! Now, it is best to rid her of her hair, vermillion, bangles, finery, and ornaments; destroy them in the way she has destroyed her husband.'

While the women stood there, spewing hatred, a man wearing rough clothes entered the backyard silently. Seeing him, the women opened the door to the inside, calling out aloud: 'Now, come out, you! Take down the weight of that arrogance you carry on your head.'

But there was no answer to the women's call. Then one of them said: 'Take him inside! Why humiliate her in public? What is the use of that now? Whatever has happened cannot be changed. She cannot help it now.'

Calling out to the servant, the women asked him to guide the newcomer, the barber Khandu, to wait inside. But though they searched the whole house, the widow was nowhere to be seen. Thinking she must be hiding out of fear, the search was abandoned. Khandu was asked to return the next day. Vinayak too returned to his own house and told Yamuna everything. As soon as she heard the news, Yamuna shuddered with fright and began crying with fear about what would befall her young friend. She would be tonsured now.

Yamuna said to Vinayak: 'These people are so cruel! Poor Godu! Why are they so hellbent on disfiguring and torturing her? I cannot imagine her plight! How will I face her now? It was just yesterday that I saw her all beautifully dressed up, and even adjusted her ornaments. Oh, what must she be going through! A mountain of troubles has collapsed onto her. Now, they will remove her bangles, they will take away her ornaments, and disfigure her. How awful! Not only does she have to bear the loss and pain of her husband's death, but additionally, she now has to bear the humiliation of being blamed and punished for it. How will she ever find the strength? Our women's lives are useless, and devoid of any happiness that we may call our own! Now, poor, widowed Godu will be abused and treated like a burden. She will remain dependent on her husband's family till her last days. In contrast, I must say I am lucky that God has given me you. I am happy and grateful for your support, protection, and loving company. I cannot live without you, even for a minute now, and I cannot imagine what agony widows undergo—at least till they meet another life companion.'

While Vinayak and Yamuna slept that night, their

heartless neighbours, unconcerned for the missing widow, even though it had grown dark outside, went off to sleep. But as the family servant went to bathe at the well, for he had accidentally touched the barber, he became suddenly alarmed at finding jasmine flowers floating on the water's surface visible in the light of his lantern.

He began wondering: There are no celebrations at this time of the year. And definitely not at home right now. Had some children thrown flowers into the well? But why would they do that? Were they playing a prank? But then he remembered—hadn't he bought Godavari-*bai* a similar flower garland yesterday? How did those flowers land up here? Had she fallen in accidentally? Half-dead by the news of her husband's death? And tortured by her sister-in-law's harsh, condemning words? Had she felt trapped enough to jump in? She could hardly have returned to her brother; he lived too far away. The neighbours would have hardly rescued her either. Oh God! What terrible turmoil she must have suffered. Oh, these stupid Brahmins! Would tonsuring a poor widow bring back her husband? He felt an alarming certainty that she had jumped into the well.

He lamented: 'You cruel, cruel well! How can you bear to hold my poor mistress inside your belly? The meek, kind, and docile child that she was!'

She had often inquired after his wife and children,

and looked after them when he was away in the city to fetch the master. She was generous too, giving his wife the finer among her old sarees. But now, what was to be done? What if she had indeed committed suicide? Whom should he tell the others? The loyal servant was lost in thought, undecided what to do. His knees shook with the shock of his discovery, and he tottered into the house. At a loss for words, and feeling weak, he could hardly articulate the unbearably painful news. Still, he went to his room crying, and confided his worries in one of the ladies of the house. But she retorted angrily, scornfully asking why that witch would now commit suicide herself, after her aim of killing her husband had been successful! The witch was simply hiding somewhere, and would be discovered tomorrow. It wasn't important enough to start searching for her in the dark now.

The issue thus remained unresolved for the night. The next morning, as they prepared to search again, someone saw her swollen, bloated corpse floating on the water's surface inside the well. A commotion broke out, and news of the girl's suicide reached the local administrator. He arranged for the body to be pulled out, and initiated inquiries into the possible reasons of her suicide. The letter that Vinayak had also been given to read was produced, and the reason for the suicide was revealed as the girl's terror of being tonsured.

3
Venu's Story

The trauma of her friend's suicide cast a dark shadow over Yamuna, even though she knew that it was God, who finally decided everyone's fate. There was no use of worrying! She tried to console herself, and gradually picked up the old threads again. In a few days, however, a new opportunity presented itself. She would soon be accompanying her husband on a long-distance business trip.

Soon after that, the couple set off for Nagpur. But they had to halt at a village on their way, because one of their servants fell ill during the journey. The entourage, thus, took up temporary residence with a Brahmin family in that village, and Vinayak arranged to have their meals with the family. With time, Yamuna became friendly with this family and began spending her free time with the women folk of the household. She learned their names, and entertained them by showing them pictures of modern machines and new technological devices from scientific books and magazines. She regaled them with wonderful stories about modern inventions in simplified language. Yamuna grew especially fond of the three daughters of that family, and they grew fond of her in return. Soon, she was everyone's favourite, and even neighbourhood women flocked to meet her, praising her for her intelligence.

Among all the women, however, there was one who was persistently excluded. Yamuna marked the absence of a young girl, Venu, who must not have been older than twenty. Venu always went around looking crestfallen and depressed. While other women smiled and laughed, she was listless and devoid of happiness. Other women wore finery and expensive ornaments, but Venu was clad in roughly-sewn, plain widow's garments. No one thought of including her among the other women flocking around Yamuna. Even if she crept up to listen and participate, someone would call to her in loud, reprimanding, and admonishing tones, and she would scurry away. As Venu's persistent exclusion became conspicuous, Yamuna began looking for opportunities to talk to her. This soon presented itself, as the whole family went one evening to visit a travelling fair. They left Vinayak and Yamuna alone at home.

Sitting in Vinayak's embrace, Yamuna suddenly heard the sound of clothes being washed in the backyard. Startled, and afraid that thieves might have entered the house through the back door, Yamuna ran to look for the source of the sound. Who could it be, she wondered. As far as she knew, Vinayak and she were alone at home. Running to the backyard, Yamuna found exactly the person she had been looking for. Venu sat there washing clothes.

Yamuna: 'Venu-*tai*, didn't you go to the fair?'

Venu just sat there looking startled, sad, and embarrassed: 'Are you really, talking to me Yamuna-*bai*? Showing me respect by calling me *tai*—the most wretched creature in this household? I am but a servant.'

Yamuna: 'Please don't say that Venu-*tai*! I mean it sincerely—not sarcastically. I feel genuine affection for you. Why do you always look so sad?'

Venu: 'I am a poor, doomed orphan, and all those who loved and protected me once are now dead and gone.'

Yamuna: 'I couldn't find the chance to talk to you earlier. I feel awkward now, speaking so directly to you in our first meeting. Please excuse my boldness.'

Venu: 'You are too kind! Please ask me anything. I will do whatever you want.'

Yamuna: 'I don't want you to do anything for

me. But won't you keep your work aside for a moment? Come, sit next to me Venu-*tai*, and tell me your story.'

Venu: 'Why do you Yamuna-*bai*, a lady so resplendent and respectable, want to know my sad, unfortunate story? What will you gain from it?'

But when Yamuna insisted, Venu finished her washing and came inside. Giving Yamuna a stool, she sat on the floor and immediately began weeping. Yamuna too, was overcome with Venu's pain.

Yamuna: 'How many people are there in your family, Venu-*tai*?'

Venu: 'Now, after my husband has passed away, I have no family left. I am a nobody!'

Yamuna: 'But where are your parents?'

Venu: 'My home is far away in Khandesh and my mother died when I was little. My father had a government job, and often had to journey to different villages. There was no one at home to look after me, and so I was married off at the age of six. Because I did not have a mother, my father did not invite me home too often either. But as if to compensate for this, my husband's grandmother, who was very fond of me, brought me up extra lovingly. She would bathe and feed me, comb my hair, and I would sleep next to her at night. She loved me so much that I never missed my mother. Later, I began living as a wife with the man I was married off to. But he too, was kind, and showered me with love. He never let the slightest unhappiness touch me. In fact, he would worry if I even caught a cold! Once when I fell ill, he sat near my bed for three nights, and arranged for the best medicines and food. Now, when I think back on those beautiful days, my blood almost dries up with grief. In my current state, no one will care to look even if I lie dying somewhere.'

Yamuna: 'Since when has all this been happening?'

Venu: 'It's been six years now that I am widowed!'

Yamuna: 'What was wrong with your husband?'

Venu: 'To tell the truth, Yamuna-*bai*, his illness was never diagnosed. He was sick for three months with a mysterious illness. His stomach would swell up into a large ball every night—so big that it nearly touched his throat. He could hardly breathe, and would start choking, and become delirious. This went on for three months, till he finally passed away.' Venu could no longer continue. Her grief overcame her, and tears streamed down her cheeks.

Yamuna: 'Poor, dear Venu-*tai*! Those three months must have weighed on you like three years.'

Venu: 'It was the very opposite Yamuna-*bai*! Those three months went by in a whirl. What should I say? I could not even find a minute to sit next to him or comfort him. My back felt like it was yoked to an enormous burden that I had to pull alone to keep him alive. I could hardly cope with my own life in that time. First, at dawn, I was to bathe in ice-cold water, and still dripping from it, circumambulate the household *tulsi* for an hour. It exhausted me, making me feel dizzy and faint. Before eight in the morning, I was supposed to go to the nearby Maruti temple, and circle the *pipal* tree outside it, a hundred and eight times. The extreme heat made my head reel. Returning home, I was instructed to cook rice-husk gruel without salt, and, disallowed from using a plate, had to eat it off the floor smeared with cow dung. In the evening, I was told to eat dry *bhakri* with its flour kneaded in cow urine. This went on for seven days, but did my husband feel any better? No! Then an astrologer was consulted to check his horoscope. The astrologer diagnosed my husband's illness to be the result of Mars affliction. Then, ritual donations were made to Mars. Many solutions were suggested, but to no avail! I would say in those days that I would undergo any ordeal just to see my husband cured. But the power of my marriage ties and *mangalsutra* proved too weak. Who could help me! When at last, I found some free time, I would sit next to him. But at such times, he would pant with exertion, and we could only look mutely and helplessly at each other. Even if I talked, he could only answer with difficulty. Those were anxious, whirlwind days, and then, suddenly, the huge calamity of his death came crashing down on me like a boulder.'

Yamuna: 'How did everyone treat you then?'

Venu: 'Oh, don't ask that Yamuna-*bai*. You have observed me since the day you arrived—well, that is how I am treated! In the first month of widowhood, I was disallowed from touching anything. Then, all the good and expensive clothes I had were taken away, and locked up in a trunk by my mother-in-law. My father-in-law took away all my jewellery that included my mother's expensive ornaments, and locked it up in his safe. My clothes and jewellery were given away to my sisters-in-law. A high-quality wooden blackwood box my father had presented me, in which I kept my mirror, combs, cosmetics, sweets, and small gifts, was taken away by my mother-in-law, and sent off to her daughter. I cried and protested but no one paid any attention. My mother-in-law said I was not allowed to possess anything from now on, and since I had no children of my own, what harm was there in sending the box elsewhere? An expensive brocade Khandeshi shawl that my brother had gifted me, is now being used by my father-in-law. How can I ever express the extent of this humiliation? I am like an orphaned cow, abandoned in the tiger's lair. People attack me from all sides, and everyone and anyone in this household exerts their power over me. I am just a servant, who slogs from dawn till late in the night, and is sent off to work with other servants, and not treated like a family member. My husband has five sisters, and whenever they visit, they each stay for two months at a time. Three of them have four children each, who constantly demand sweetmeats. All the extra burden falls on me, and I am additionally charged with helping my sisters-in-law draw warm water baths, combing and decorating their hair, washing their clothes, cleaning their leftovers after mealtimes, and smearing the floor with cow dung three times a day. It is only on festivals that I ever get a piece of sweetmeat, and that too, if it is a leftover, and already stale and rancid. If I refuse to eat stale food, I am insulted and abused—called a stubborn, arrogant mule.'

Yamuna: 'Do you have enough clothes?'

Venu: 'Clothes are the biggest difficulty! Since I am disallowed from sleeping on a bed, I must sleep on the stone floor on a blanket and a tattered shawl. I have three or four old sarees, and a coarse woollen covering. And that is the end of all my possessions. For three nights in a month, I have to sleep on the cold floor, without a blanket. There was a time, Yamuna-*bai*, when I gave people gifts. Now, no one gives me a penny. There is an older sister-in-law, who gives me money and arranges for food whenever she visits, but that is only once every year or six months. That is only fleeting comfort. Once she is gone, I am back where I began. How long should I carry on in this wretched story! No one speaks a kind word to me. Though the day-time passes in work, and the night-time in sleeping like a corpse, I awaken early at times and start thinking: what is the use of continuing like this? I should end my life by jumping into a well or a pond, and be free of this burden once and for all. But then again, the hope of better times also continues to persist. How unlucky I am! I wish I had never been born! I hope I die!'

Yamuna: 'My heart breaks for you, dear Venu-*tai*. If it were in my hands, I would have relieved you of your difficulties. But I am helpless. May God shower you with mercy. I know He is mighty enough to fill your heart with peace and satisfaction. Please have faith. God is father to all orphans, and husband to all widows. He will hear your cry.'

Venu: 'What is left for God to do now? How can He improve my state? If He had truly loved me, would He have ever let me suffer so? Why should I ask Him for anything now? He has already decided my fate! It is only to preserve my parents' reputation that I desist from committing suicide. But once I die, no one will ever ask.'

Yamuna: 'Venu-*tai*, please don't think of committing suicide. It is a sin.'

Venu: 'What do I care for sin or merit now? God has turned His back on me, and my life is living hell. What is the use of this life?'

Yamuna: 'Please Venu-*tai*, don't think like that!'

Venu: 'Then what do you suggest I do, Yamuna-*bai*? Do you know of another way out?'

Yamuna: 'If I had any say in the matter, I would have put a stop to your suffering this minute. But I am an outsider in this household. I can only pray and ask God to bless you, and have compassion for you. May He remove all the difficulties in your path and impart you happiness. Also, Venu-*tai*, I have a few things to gift you.'

Venu: 'Wait! If it is clothes, then it will never reach me. I am not allowed to wear good clothes, and if gifted anything, I have to deposit it with my mother-in-law.'

Yamuna: 'I will make arrangements with your in-laws, and request them to allow you to keep the things I give you.'

Venu: 'But how and where shall I keep these things? Do I even own a box? Or a corner that I could call my own? I am homeless, an orphan! Even cows have cowsheds, but not me. I don't have any place to call my own.'

Yamuna began thinking, if Venu-*tai* were to know about Jesus Christ, perhaps it would comfort her. She would focus her hope and pray thus: God, when you decided to take birth as a human being, you too found no place on earth! Should I tell her His story? Would she receive it with a positive heart and an open mind? On the other hand, would the poor thing even understand what I am saying? She must never have even heard of Christ. But then, God has Himself promised that He is like the rain from the heavens that accords the planter his seeds and the hungry his food. Yamuna thought that this was perhaps an ideal opportunity to tell Venu about her own secret religion.

Yamuna: 'Venu-*tai*, I want to tell you a secret. Though I identify as a Hindu woman in public, in my heart, I believe in a different religion. I am convinced that my religion is true, and the only way in which I will find God. Even though my beliefs are yet a secret, my mind has undergone a sea-change since I have recognized my true religion. Though I know I am a sinner and a criminal, and should be punished and sent to hell, God has opened my eyes and shown me the way forward, to redeem myself of sin, seek forgiveness, and purify my heart. I hope God gives me strength to proclaim my true religion openly. I will tell you about it, since I think this is the best solution for your troubles. God sent us His only, beloved son, Jesus Christ, incarnated as a human being on earth, with the aim of redeeming us of sin. This son of God suffered untold agonies, taking all the burden of human sins upon His head. He was crucified, died for mankind's sins, and rose again. His death served an important purpose of redeeming mankind of the sins that God felt angry with humans about. So, whoever believes in this redeemer Lord Jesus Christ, his sins are automatically forgiven and washed away. The holy and pure spirit of God enters him and accords him a completely new personality as well as a new heart different from the old. The Holy Spirit imbues the believer with purity, serenity, and satisfaction and gives him strength to bear sorrows, difficulties, and torture, and this strengthens the believer's love and faith in God. Venu-*tai*, if you accept this truth, then I promise you, your life of drudgery will be completely transformed, allowing you to feel blissful even amidst terrible suffering.'

Venu: 'If this is true, then my next question is, how will this God come here? If this God had really been here, then why would He make me suffer so much?'

Yamuna: 'He is constantly with us Venu-*tai*. In fact, Lord Jesus Christ calls out to all those suffering like you, saying: "Oh, those of you suffering and burdened, come closer to me and I will relieve you." Aren't those sweet, kind, and comforting words?'

Venu: 'Yes, He sounds so kind! If I were indeed to find this God, I would go running to Him. I have no hope of ever finding succour here. I know, the household here will work me to the bone, and I will finally die a beast of burden. But where is this God? If I only knew where to find Him, it would become so much simpler!'

Yamuna: 'But Venu-*tai*, I have just told you, God is already here.'

Venu: 'What? Here? Right now? But how can I see Him? Why don't you point Him out to me? After finding Him, I will never leave His feet again. I will beg Him to free me of my sorrows, starting with the task of grinding grain tonight with the other servants. Wait! Could it be that you are that God? I fall at your feet then, Yamuna-*bai*. Please save me. I am tired of this awful drudgery. Look at my swollen back! Yesterday, my brother-in-law beat me black and blue with an umbrella stick for no fault of mine. See the weal of that thrashing! I was too ashamed to show you earlier.' Venu began to cry. 'What should I say? I have to bear everything here in silence and keep working. There is no one to talk to, or call my own. Now, you have heard everything. Now, you decide whether to kill me or spare me. Where else shall I find justice?'

Yamuna began to feel very bad for Venu—not only for her torture, but also for her abysmal state of ignorance about God's nature.

She said: 'Venu-*tai*, please don't be afraid. Also, I am no God or healer. In the abject condition you are in, I doubt whether your sorrows will disappear overnight. But please continue to hold strongly to faith. Look to God and pray with faith in your heart. He is kind and just. Even though you are suffering injustice and feeling hopeless, have faith. The king of heaven is tremendously strong, and you must remember, He is by your side as a witness. On judgement day, He will give us all our just returns, but your rewards may not come so easily unless you keep strong faith in Jesus Christ. All your past and your present suffering, and the days ahead that seem bleak, have overwhelmed you, and you are waiting for that one ray of light that will show you the way forward out of this suffering. You will walk on that path shown by God, even if it is full of thorns and stones. Your road to happiness must first traverse through difficulties, and only after transcending these, will you achieve happiness. Our Lord Jesus Christ, the only and beloved son of God asks us to be faithful. He says: "At the time you cross the water, I will stand next to you. At the time you cross rivers, I will ensure you don't drown. And at the time you walk through fire, I will ensure you are not burned. I am your God, and I have come to you from Israel, to redeem you of your suffering.'"

Venu did not understand this last part. But still, she tried to believe what Yamuna was telling her, as she was desperate with suffering. Taking permission from her husband, Yamuna thereafter presented Venu with some clothes, assuring her that these wouldn't be taken away. She promised to arrange this with her mother-in-law. In a few days, as their servant's health improved, Vinayak and Yamuna resumed their journey to Nagpur. Yamuna told Vinayak about Venu, and commented on how much better it would have been if widows were allowed to remarry. If families persisted in disallowing widow-remarriage, what would happen to women like Venu? Venu's suffering broke Yamuna's heart, but there was no way out of it either. It would be ideal if Venu remarried. She had become so terrified of the future that she had lost all hope. The seemingly endless suffering of life had petrified and paralyzed her. Yamuna told Vinayak about recounting Lord Jesus Christ's story to Venu, and about how Venu had listened with all her heart. They both prayed: 'May God's words find a place in Venu's heart, growing there into a tree of support, that would bestow her with the fruits of happiness.'

4

The Imposter's Disguise

Vinayak-*rao* and Yamuna-*bai* reached Nagpur in the next week, and Yamuna began making new friendships there, with people being naturally attracted to her sweet nature. Vinayak soon became engrossed in work, often returning home late at night. He, too, befriended a wealthy young man from the Maratha caste. This man was 'reformed', and having studied at an English missionary school, Vinayak and he agreed on many matters. They often held long discussions on many matters of mutual interest. One night on their way home, the friends, walking leisurely through the grass, admired the clear sky, the bright moonlight that had turned the world into silver, and the stars that glimmered like diamonds in the sky. However, just as the heady fragrance of flowers from nearby gardens wafted over them in the cool, gentle, late-evening breeze, a snake suddenly accosted them out of nowhere. Startled, they stopped in their tracks, and having no weapons to defend themselves, retreated hastily, and changed direction. Daulat-*rao*, Vinayak's new friend, remarked that God had indeed saved them from an unimaginable and terrible fate.

Vinayak: 'God has saved us today, *dada*! He cares for us every minute of the day and night, and keeps to the promise offered by the Christian scriptures that assures us that believers need not dread the night. If that snake had bitten us, and if we had died, what on earth would have happened to our wives? My poor dear wife would have become a widowed in a foreign land, far from home. Who would have looked after her here? *Dada*, to tell you the truth, the worry of what will transpire if I were to suddenly pass away, plagues me constantly and fills my heart with anxiety and pain. What can I do? When will I ever be free of this worry! What will happen to our women?'

Daulat: 'If I had died today, my wife, too, would have been condemned to a life of unending widowhood.'

Vinayak: 'Why condemned? Are Maratha widows prohibited from remarrying?'

Daulat: 'Maybe the poorer families remarry their widows, but elite Maratha families emulate Brahminical practices and would therefore not dream of remarrying their widows.'

The Imposter's Disguise

Vinayak: 'What madness this is! Why? Oh, when will people learn! It is a terrible mistake to assume that following Brahmin rituals confers everyone with high status. In reality, it just invites trouble.'

Daulat: 'Doubtless! Our caste has been almost destroyed in recent times due to such emulations, in a rift caused by animosity and antagonism over the refusal to remarry widows.'

Vinayak: 'How? What happened?'

Daulat: 'See, my maternal uncle has three daughters. Now, his middle daughter became widowed within a year of her marriage, and he thereafter brought her back home. He was affluent, and so, she did not lack anything. In fact, she was treated very lovingly. Her father had great compassion for her, and would shower her with gifts. Despite this, the pain of widowhood kept tormenting her, and she grew pale and thin. Her sadness grew unbearable especially during any celebrations at home. At such occasions, she would mope, wear her widow's garb, sit in a corner, sob, and cry. This pained her father terribly, as he was unable to alleviate her suffering.'

Vinayak: 'Oh, the poor thing! I feel such pity for her.'

Daulat: 'It would have been fine if the matter had stopped at that.'

Vinayak: 'Why? What happened?'

Daulat: 'On someone's advice, my uncle decided to turn his daughter's attention towards a spiritual path. Since she was herself illiterate, he hired a priest who would come home every day to read out the Bhagwat Puran to her. But this had the opposite effect! That priest, understanding her weakness, began reading out portions of the text that described Krishna's sexual dalliance with milkmaids, and their erotic escapades. Listening to this lessened my cousin's grief alright, instead generating in her the new desire to remarry. At the time when this allegedly holy act of reading erotic materials was in full swing, a famous ascetic arrived in town. He soon became popular and everyone began discussing his miracles. Women, and that too women from elite Maratha families, who seldom step outside the house, began visiting this ascetic to seek his blessings.'

'My uncle, too, took it into his head to take his widowed daughter to the ascetic. He hoped her mind would turn to prayer, and that she would find solace in spiritual life. He had always been naïve, and now, his love and worry for his beloved, widowed daughter had blinded him. My uncle believed whatever people told him—lies spread by this ascetic's disciples, for example—about how the ascetic had the power of healing women, simply by placing his hand on their heads. He believed in stories about the ascetic's alleged fame—about how the ascetic was the grandson of the proclaimed Baba Chidanand from Paithan. It was said that the deity Vithoba himself had once garlanded Baba Chidanand, feeling overjoyed at hearing the latter's *kirtan*. My uncle, his mind full of all these fake stories, set off with his daughter to meet the ascetic. As expected, this first meeting was soon followed by other meetings, after which my cousin began attending special worship ceremonies and *puja*s that were held at night.'

Vinayak: 'What kind of ascetic was he?'

Daulat: 'None at all! He was an imposter. He disguised himself as an ascetic only to dupe others. I became suspicious right at the beginning when my cousin started going to him. But no one paid any heed to my warning. This charlatan's popularity was rising on the other hand, and in the subsequent months of *chaturmasa*, my cousin began staying at his house till late in the night, presumably for attending these *puja* ceremonies. The ascetic, sometimes, accompanied by other female devotees, commenced with goddess worship rituals at midnight, and my foolish uncle felt relieved that his daughter was finally healed and had turned to a spiritual path. Many days passed thus, till *dussehra*, after which the ascetic suddenly absconded. This in turn brought tremendous shame and humiliation to my uncle—a man of some standing of our caste in the village.'

Vinayak: 'Why? Did the widowed daughter do something?'

Daulat: 'That ascetic mesmerized and charmed her so much that she ran away with him, and stole goods worth one-and-a-half-thousand rupees from home before doing so. The goons of the ascetic, disguised as his disciples, were immediately arrested and imprisoned, but they had to be released as there was no sound evidence against them. My cousin, however, was lost forever.'

Vinayak: 'This is extremely sad. Her father pampered her and foolishly gave in to her every whim! And this only led her to fall prey to criminals. If instead, he had got her remarried, these difficulties would have been averted. He would not have faced shame or humiliation either. Now, having fallen on immoral ways, her life must be unimaginably difficult.'

Daulat: 'Yes, this charlatan will keep her till the money lasts, and then, he will abandon her somewhere. His so-called disciples, after being arrested, confessed that he had done the same thing to other girls before. It was his specialty—reducing vulnerable women from good families to beggars.'

Vinayak: 'What happened then?'

Daulat: 'What else? She never returned, and her departure drove a wedge through our community. Despite strict taboos followed by our Maratha women, my uncle had allowed his daughter to repeatedly visit this ascetic alone, and at night, and he had been wrong in doing so as he had been grievously duped. The caste council decided to fine my uncle, placing an indemnity on him of feeding the entire community as a form of reparation. My cousin's disappearance and elopement had after all caused a collective loss of dignity to our caste. But since my uncle refused to comply, they excommunicated him, along with the family and other associates.'

Vinayak: 'What is your opinion about your caste after this event?'

Daulat: 'What should I say, *dada*! Sorrow meets the eye everywhere one looks. As the Prophet Joshua said, all heads are bent in sorrow, and each heart is besieged with sickness. Not one sign of wellbeing—only bodies full of scars, scabs, and bleeding wounds. No one to soothe or bandage them! The superstitions of my caste define and preoccupy them, and this has led to their own downfall. No one considers the consequences of their action. The few who do, lead an entirely different life. Sadly, although there are many young and educated men who support widow-remarriage, none have come forward to marry widows.'

Vinayak: 'I have heard that Maratha widows, especially from this Nagpur region are promiscuous? Is it true?'

Daulat: 'Though I am ashamed of it, I must say that it is true! My community is strict and has never practised widow-remarriage. This has led many widows into secret and immoral sexual alliances. But if a widow starts a secret liaison, her parents or in-laws don't even care enough to reprimand her. They just poison her and kill her.'

Vinayak: 'What? What are you saying, *dada*! Openly murder her? Do people of your caste seriously go around murdering widows in the family and community? Oh my God! This is terrible indeed!'

Daulat: 'Yes, it is shocking, and also painfully true! The huge Maratha mansions you see around here, all harbour secret inner chambers—a private, hidden den of dark tunnels that hides the secrets of family sins—bodies of murdered women hidden there. Even police officers find it difficult to bring their remains to light.'

Vinayak: 'I have only read about such terrible things in old books—mostly in the context of inquisitions, the torture chambers of the Spanish, and the prisons of Roman Catholic countries. But I did not dream of it being the same over here. Don't people realize how cruel and wrong this is?'

Daulat: 'Everyone knows about these cruel and criminal deeds, but no one wants to talk, lest it discredits the community and compromises Maratha status. *Dada*, you are surprised only because you don't know Maratha traditions. I, on the other hand, have good knowledge of all such practices. Two years back in Mumbai, when a high-caste widow became pregnant after having an affair, she first pretended to be ill and did not leave home, and then, accompanied by a male relative, who was also her paramour, she travelled to another village on the pretext of recouping. There she gave birth, and promptly gave the child to a maidservant to raise. But when their other accompanying servant, a small boy from Mumbai with them, came to know of their secret, the couple became afraid that he would gossip. So, they murdered him, returning to Mumbai and pretending that he had accidentally drowned. Another tragic instance was of a widow from the Shenoy caste. The Shenoys also imitate Brahmins by disallowing their women from remarrying. This nine-year-old Shenoy widow from Mumbai came to realize the implications of widowhood only after attaining puberty. She then expressed the desire to remarry. Hearing this, a distant male relative invited her home and professed his sympathy. He asked her to marry him, despite being married already. Moreover, she immediately agreed to the proposal. When her parents came to know of it and asked her to explain, demanding that she protect family reputation by turning him down, she flatly refused. Instead, she reiterated her intention to marry him, though he was already married. Her enraged parents thrashed her, took away her things, and began torturing her, first through the instrument of a caste-gathering that humiliated and condemned her, and then, by imprisoning her in a subterranean, dark cellar full of noxious fumes. They fed her through a small hole in the wall. She remained that way for many days, locked up like an animal in a cage. But how long could the torture have lasted? It had to end some day! After a while, they let her go, and she promptly returned to her immoral and deceitful paramour, and began living with him openly in sin.'

Vinayak: 'How terribly shocking! When he was already married, why did he give her false hopes about marrying her? That only forced her to live an immoral life. Had he really cared for her, he would have married her off to a young, unmarried man.'

Soon, the friends arrived at home. Leaving their conversation midway, they bid each other farewell. As a result of the conversation, Vinayak became deeply aware of the suffering of widows, and began worrying ceaselessly for his wife. What would become of her if he preceded her in death?

5
The Wig

Yamuna's health began deteriorating within a year of their travels. She soon became so ill and weak that doctors advised her to leave Nagpur till the time she recovered. The couple was forced to return to southern Maharashtra, and after trying out cities like Amravati, Nanded, Naladurg, and Solapur, they finally halted in Pandharpur, as Yamuna grew too weak to travel any further. For a couple of months, they took up residence as tenants at the home of a Brahmin widow, and arranged to have their meals with her. Since her house was located outside town, it was away from crowds, and in the fresh air. The widow lived alone with her eleven-year-old son, Shivram, and the boy spent his days begging in the town, telling people tales that he was a hungry orphan whose mother had drowned in the Chandrabhaga River.

He would cheat pilgrims and extract free rations

of rice, pulses, flour, butter, cash, and old clothes from them. And on days when begging did not elicit much, he pilfered and stole, afraid that his mother would beat him, or refuse him food if he returned home empty handed. Since Yamuna was initially still unwell, Vinayak did not find the time to notice these small things about Shivram and his mother. But their problems could not evade his attention for much longer. Yamuna, by God's grace, began gradually to recover and Vinayak was tremendously relieved.

Once, as they both sat discussing her health, Yamuna said: 'My dear, God has been so kind to me by helping me to recover from my illness. While so many thousands succumb, I am still alive and well. We must secure God's continued blessings. What do you think we should do? For my part, I feel undeserving of such a beautiful world. I feel unworthy of enjoyment. I am a sinner and only deserve to be punished. We have broken so many of God's commandments, and it is only right that he should be angry with us. Every time I think of it, my heart fills with fear. I cannot tell you how afraid I felt when I fell ill. I incessantly prayed to my redeemer to save me. Though I had faith in him, I also repented for not following God's commandments. I wondered how he would ever forgive my sins and pardon my trespasses.'

Hearing this, Vinayak said: 'My dear, I am deeply

grateful to God for healing you. I think God sends us illnesses with a purpose. He disciplines us with loving kindness, just as a gardener prunes the plants in his garden. This is for the plant's own good, so that it should bear better fruit in the future.'

Yamuna asked: 'Is that true? But if we are really the plants in His garden, then He could also break us down for disobeying him—so many of us live fearlessly in sin for years, uncaring that we never bear fruit! This is a terrible sin, and even the thought of it fills my heart with terror.'

Vinayak answered: 'We must be grateful to God, for giving us this spiritual awareness. Look at the people around us! There are millions, to whom these thoughts never occur. Some languish in illness for years; others waste time in making ritual wishes and offerings to stone idols; others seek useless advice from priests, influential persons, or officers, while yet others organize ceremonies and temple festivals. That we have both been saved from such foolish superstitions, and have instead turned to the true path of devotion—the *bhakti marga* that God has shown us is evidence enough of his mercy upon us. It is true, we are unable to follow completely in the path He has laid out; and certainly, we are to blame for it. But let us hope that God continues to shower his benevolence and mercy upon us, giving us the strength to take our next steps in the right direction, like in the way he has brought us here.'

Yamuna said: 'My dearest husband, I am overcome with sadness at the miseries all around. Even if we were to take the example of the woman in whose house we currently stay; I suffer greatly from her artificial rituals and idol worship. She understands nothing about God and moreover, behaves immorally. I feel suspicious of her conduct. I see a married woman every day, dressed in an ornate saree, leaving the house at night. Who could she be? And how is she connected to our landlady?'

Vinayak confirmed that he too had seen this married lady dressed in finery entering the house every day at dawn. He had not been able to recognize her. Vinayak and Yamuna decided to ask their landlady about this woman.

Yamuna asked their landlady the next day: '*Bai*, who is the married lady visiting this house every day?'

Looking startled, the landlady denied it at first, saying there was no one else in the house but for themselves. But when Yamuna persisted, saying that she had often seen this lady, sometimes in a white brocade saree, and at times in an ornate *Chandrakala*, the landlady grew flustered and answered: 'Yamuna-*bai*, you must have had a divine vision of the goddess Rakhma-*mai*. She is the main goddess of our household shrine, and very potent. It is she who comes home every morning to visit me, and then stays with me the entire day. She dislikes the crowds that throng at the main temple of Vithoba, and unable to tolerate the chaos, escapes and comes here instead. When the crowds dissipate at night, she returns to her husband Vithoba at the temple.'

Yamuna found the landlady's story unconvincing. But since she was unable to unravel the mystery any further, she kept quiet. When she told her husband about it, they decided to investigate the matter further. But before doing so, Vinayak first asked Shivram about the lady. He was young, and might tell the truth! But if Shivram too failed to shed any light on the matter, Vinayak resolved to directly confront their landlady. Discovering Shivram in the veranda tying his turban one evening, Vinayak began questioning him.

Vinayak: 'Hello, Shivram! Where are you off to, wearing such a fine turban?'

Shivram: 'I am supposed to accompany the chariot procession today.'

Vinayak: 'What chariot procession?'

Shivram: 'Don't you know? The Vithoba chariot procession this evening? I may earn some money at the rituals there. A rich businessman has organized an extravagant ceremony. Won't you attend it?'

Vinayak: 'Ok! Let us change the subject. Tell me, do you have any sisters?'

Shivram: 'My mother and I are alone here, and I have no siblings. I am my mother's only child.'

Vinayak: 'Do other women visit here?'

Shivram: 'Why should other women visit? Which other women? Do you mean the ones who sometimes come here after their bath at the Chandrabhaga?'

Vinayak: 'What about the married lady who goes out of this house every night?'

Shivram: 'I really don't know anything about that!'

Vinayak-*rao*'s suspicion deepened. This was awkward. He could hardly walk up to an unknown married lady and ask her questions! He would have to set a trap for her, if he wanted to catch her red-handed. Vinayak had a sudden brainwave. He decided to lock the front door from the outside once the mysterious married lady left. Carrying out his plan, he placed a lock on the front door, and re-entering from the back, locked the back door from inside. At dawn, the married woman, as usual, her head covered with one end of her saree, hurried up to the house. But finding the front door locked from outside, she grew flustered and headed to the back door that Vinayak had bolted from inside.

Unable to enter the house from the back door, the woman grew panic stricken. As Vinayak watched in silent bewilderment, she hurried into the adjacent cowshed and was just taking off and hiding the wig that covered her head, when Vinayak accosted her. Realizing that her game was over, and not finding another escape, the woman fell at Vinayak's feet and began begging: 'Please, sir. Please save my life and forgive me! I know I am a sinner, and I abjectly ask for your forgiveness.'

As soon as he heard the voice, Vinayak immediately recognized her as none other than their landlady. He asked incredulously: 'Is it really you who enters the house at dawn every day? Where do you go every night?'

The landlady answered: 'Please, sir. Please don't humiliate me any further by asking questions. You have caught me red-handed! What more do you want? And how does it matter? I suffer my fate alone. When I came to this town, I was too poor to feed myself and my child. I have been roaming from one town to another with my child for many years, and all the people I met, only exploited me. No one offered me any kindness or support. I was, after all, a young widow, and alone with a child. They set me on an immoral path for their own avarice and cruel enjoyment. Now, what is the use of even regretting all of that?'

Vinayak-*rao*: 'I am surprised that a person as thoughtful as you should ever stoop so low, to such a sinful life!'

Lady: 'There is nothing surprising about it. Once you hear my story, you will understand my life better.'

It was broad daylight by now, and Vinayak allowed the lady to enter the house from the back. He also retrieved her wig. It was a clever thing woven out of actual hair, and once worn over the head, it sat there tightly like a cap, transforming a widow into a married woman. In fact, this was the very aim of that contraption—to disguise widows.

After finishing their food and ablutions, Vinayak and Yamuna decided to leave the lady's house and move to another residence. They did not want to continue staying in what was after all an immoral household. But since they were unable to arrange for a new residence immediately, they had to wait a while. Besides, Vinayak was curious about the landlady's story. In the evening, the couple called upon the lady to settle their dues, saying: '*Bai*, we stayed here only because we did not know about your life. But now, we find it inappropriate and improper to continue staying here. The only thing we want to advise you before leaving is to repent your sins and leave this immoral path.'

The lady said: 'Sir, I only request you to listen to my story. What you say is true, and you are also right to blame me. But if you were to hear my story, and of how I fell on these bad ways, you will perhaps understand that my sins are not because I am a bad person. They are because I am a helpless widow.'

6

The Maidservant's Trickery

The landlady began telling her story: '*Dada*, I was from an affluent, cultured family. My father worked at the Sarkar-*wada* in Satara, and we enjoyed large fiefdoms of royal *inam* lands. I was my father's only daughter, and he was extremely fond of me. Commenting on my beauty, he would often compare me to the moon, saying that I looked like the moon's sister.

He sent Brahmins across the country to look for a suitable match for me, and these Brahmins searched far and wide and even went as far as Kashi to search for a groom for me. Finally, a suitable boy was found. He was the son of a wealthy military general of the Shinde family, and was handsome and talented. My father paid a handsome dowry of nine thousand rupees at my wedding, spending another three or four thousand on inviting relatives—giving them gifts and

The Maidservant's Trickery

paying their travel expenses. Similarly, he invited two hundred guests from my husband's side, paying their travel expenses too.

'I cannot begin to describe the splendour of my wedding ceremony. Even the Maharaja of Satara attended the wedding. The villagers were fed free of cost for an entire month, and five meals out of these were feasts. After the wedding, my father accepted my father-in-law's request and decided to send me to Gwalior along with them to their home. Though my father travelled part of the journey with us for the first two days, he had to return to Satara for work. We continued, proceeding slowly to Gwalior in a large entourage consisting of many carts. My father-in-law had his own cart, but his cart was accompanied by those of his wives, maids, other servants, and employees, who in turn, had brought their own wives, families, and children along. It was a group of more than two hundred. Unfortunately, the journey proved disastrous and we faced terrible water shortage. These were after all the arid summer months of April and May. Even the animals could not find enough water to drink. In addition, the servants had packed along the sweetmeats from the wedding feast, and crammed themselves full of this stale food constantly. The sweets especially, had already started spoiling in the heat.

'In addition, they drank unclean, muddy water,

wherever they found it. Soon, they started falling ill with stomach problems. After ten days of suffering water shortage, one of the maidservants fell violently ill with vomiting and diarrhoea. This spread panic in the rest of the group. And yet, they did not stop gorging themselves on the by-now rotten food. As a result, an epidemic broke out in our entourage, with one or two people dying every day. This spread further panic, and no one really knew what to do.

'There was a *vaidya* from the Maratha caste among us, from Kashi. He had studied in an English school and was educated. He divided our entourage into four groups, and advised each group to take a different route to Gwalior. Our part of the group wandered distant places searching for villages that could offer us water, rest, and simple food. We washed our clothes, aired out our carts and palanquins at each halt, and burned the stale food that the servants had packed. Gradually, the epidemic stemmed in our group. Later, when we arrived at the outskirts of Gwalior, esteemed persons from the city came to greet and welcome us.

'Servants from my husband's household began helping us, and their family priest was called to identify an auspicious occasion for my entry into the city. Since there was no immediate auspicious moment for the first meeting between husband and wife, we had to continue camping in the jungles outside Gwalior for the next three days. Members from other groups that had joined us by then also waited with us, under the misconception that their entry into the city was also forbidden till the right astrological time arrived for me. So, all the groups congregated again, and everybody began eating large quantities of food like earlier.

'After entering Gwalior, revelries and celebrations began in earnest. My father-in-law's friends and relatives organized week-long lavish feasts. It was amidst this endless eating that my husband developed a stomach-ache, and fell ill with violent symptoms of diarrhoea. But he did not tell anyone. After the pain grew unbearable and he started vomiting, he had to finally tell his father about it. The news spread like wildfire. Even though their family *vaidya* kept giving my husband medicine, the vomiting refused to abate. Finally, when even the *vaidya* gave up, everyone grew dismayed. Ladies in the women's quarters began weeping in advance. My husband's hands and feet gradually turned ice-cold, and he started having seizures. He could not say a single word in the end. Everyone gave up hope, and the next morning, an hour before dawn, he finally passed away.

'The grieving was endless. Everyone lamented his death and was disconsolate. It was as if the world had drowned into a sea of anguish. After a month, my father-in-law asked me whether I wanted to return home to my father in Satara, or whether I wanted to continue living in Gwalior. I was a child and hardly understood the gravity of these fast changes taking place in my life. I trusted everyone. I could not answer him properly. People in the household were of the opinion that I should stay, at least till my husband's first annual death ritual, the *varshik shraddha*. In this way, a year went by. I did not understand the import of my husband's death, and actually, did not feel any grief either. After my husband's *shraddha*, I began preparing to return to my father. But news came from Satara that my father had been accused of embezzlement and was imprisoned. So, I relinquished the plan of returning home. My father-in-law was cultured, educated, and a kind-hearted man. He did not cause me any harm. In fact, he treated me like a daughter. I resumed normal life and even began attending weddings with other family members. I remembered going to a wedding at the time with my sister-in-law, where a dance performance was specially organized for the women attendees. I had never seen dancing women before.'

'A day or two after returning from the wedding, my maidservant said to me: "Dear girl, what will you do now? In another five or six years, they will tonsure you and confiscate all your jewellery, and finery. How will you continue then?"

'I disagreed with my maidservant, asserting that my father-in-law would never let such a thing happen to me.

But she laughed: "Not only will he allow it to happen; he will oversee it. You are perhaps too young to understand all this. Didn't you know, widows are tonsured at the death of their husbands? No one has forced you so far because you are as yet a child. Now that you proceed towards puberty, do you think they will spare you the tonsuring?"

I said: "Why do you say this? Will I never find a new husband? Once I return to my father's house, I will surely remarry."

She said: "Don't even say the word 'husband' out aloud again, whether you live in Satara with your father, or whether you continue living here. Wherever you go henceforth, it is now your fate to wear rags, and busy yourself with menial household tasks."

I asked: "Then, what should I do?" She said: "If you listen carefully, I can search for a new husband for you, but only on the sly. You will only find happiness in that way now. After another six months or a year, your father-in-law will depart to Kashi on a pilgrimage. He is old and hopes to die there. After that, there will be no one left in this household to protect you. Your sisters-in-law will peck at you like crows on carrion. They already hate you, but are forced to keep quiet for fear of your father-in-law, who is fond of you. No one gives you any work at present because you are as yet not tonsured. But once the barber has a go at you with his shaving comb, your condition will be no different than the neighbourhood widow, Bhimi. It was only yesterday that your older sister-in-law was discussing your future with the family priest, and he said the first thing required was taking the weight of your hair off from your head."

When I retorted that I would return to my father, and that he would never do any injustice to me, the maidservant said: "Don't you know that your wedding has financially ruined your father? All the thousands he spent on your wedding! From where do you think he got all that money? He borrowed it from the Sarkar-*wada* treasury of course, and unable to repay the money, he is imprisoned. Dear girl, listen to me, for I have looked after you since you were a child. I find the spectre of sorrow that presently looms over you, unbearable to behold. Once you are tonsured and begin living as a widow, I too will have to leave your service and return home. Then you will regret not heeding my advice."'

'In this way my maidservant tricked me, plunging my innocent life into a well of sorrow and anxiety. And she was plausible only because of her half-truths. That is why I ended up believing her. It was true that Bhimi next door was a poor, young widow. Her mother-in-law was a monster, who made Bhimi slog like an animal and beat her black and blue. Bhimi's sisters-in-law were equally cruel. I felt miserable for Bhimi's pathetic condition, and when my maidservant said my fate would be similar, I suddenly lost faith in my father-in-law, and believed in her instead. I curse myself today, and I curse her for her trickery. The maidservant that my own mother had sent along with me to my husband's house ended up cheating me.'

7
Cheated!

'I initially thought we would wait to run away from home till after my father-in-law left for Kashi. But my maidservant convinced me that, unless we left earlier, I would lose all my ornaments. And indeed, my father-in-law did usually lock away all my expensive things in a safe before he left for any journey. Again, finding her half-truths plausible, I followed her advice. On the next new moon night, that hag took me to the stables and removed all my ornaments, saying that people would otherwise recognize me by my ornaments. She kept the ornaments with her, and telling me that we would hide in the stables for the night, and run away to meet my new husband next morning, she heated some milk for me and gave me some sweets to eat. I slept so deeply thereafter that I didn't know what else transpired. When I awoke, I was no longer in the stables, and my maidservant was gone. I was lying on a cot in a room.

'Hearing me cry out in shock and terror, an old woman came rushing over and said: "Child, don't cry! Consider this to be your new home from now on. You will get everything you need over here."'

'She brought me outside but I did not recognize anybody. Everyone was a stranger, but for two women who looked vaguely familiar. Trying to place them, I suddenly recognized them as the dancers, who had danced at the wedding I had attended a few days ago. It was then that I realized what my maidservant had done. She had cheated and kidnapped me, and sold me to a brothel. I was shocked and terrified. This had not been my intention when I had expressed the wish to remarry. I had wanted to remarry in exactly the same way that I had married the first time, and because my in-laws were discussing my younger brother-in-law's wedding, I thought they would soon find a groom for me too. Seeing that I was in a brothel, I started missing home sorely—both my childhood home as well as my in-laws' home, and wept copiously. I did not eat anything that day. In the evening, all the women dressed-up in expensive clothes and jewellery. As the evening lights came on, they began singing and dancing. I kept sitting in a corner and crying. At night, I was hungry, but I had made up my mind not to ask for anything. But the old lady from the morning came in with a plate of sweetmeats and a big bowl of milk.'

'She chided me, saying: "*Bachcha*, stop being so stubborn! Consider this your new home. It will feel a little strange for a while, but thereafter, you will forget everything and start smiling, and begin to enjoy your life. You will wear expensive clothes and ornaments and be like the other girls here. We will teach you to sing and dance too, and we will get you married. Drink up the milk now, my child, and eat up the sweets. Don't feel afraid! I will take care of you."'

'I was hungry because I had not eaten all day, and was exhausted with weeping. I drank the milk and ate the sweets, and again slept deeply. When I awoke, the room, the cot, and the old lady had again disappeared. I was inside a closed cart now that was racing ahead with tremendous speed. At first, I thought it was a dream. Then when I looked outside, I realized the truth; I was in a cart that was hurtling through the countryside at top speed, and I was helpless and trapped inside. There was nothing left for me to do but to keep lying inside. It must have been two in the afternoon when the cart finally came to a stop. We were in front of a strange mansion and the drivers took me inside. I did not even have the energy to sit. I fell into a high fever that lasted for the next eight days, and I was unable to think. Whenever I awoke I would remember my home and weep.

'After some days, when I gradually began feeling better, I asked the lady looking after me, whose house it was, and who had brought me there. The lady was very kind. She had looked after me throughout my illness, giving me medicine, food, and water, and staying awake at my bedside. She would tell me stories, entertain, and comfort me, and lull me back to sleep whenever I awoke. I had grown attached to her and my homesickness abated somewhat. The other girls in that mansion learned music every morning and evening. Initially I sat by and only listened. But gradually, I too felt like learning music. Days went by in this way. What should I say! My will was broken; I accepted my fate, and became one of those other girls. In another two or three years, I was performing songs and dances at festive occasions too, and at home, it was the same thing morning and night. After some time, I tired of it all—staying up till very late every night, learning new songs, and forever forced to make new friendships with clients. My life started oppressing me. And besides, I had no access to the money I earned. The ornaments and clothes I wore were loaned. Soon, the kind-hearted lady who cared for me passed away. There was nothing left there for me any longer and I started thinking of ways of escaping.

'A chance arrived when our music teacher, a

Brahmin by birth, decided to quit his job and return to his family in Kashi. I decided to use this opportunity. I knew he liked me, and one day I confided in him, expressing my desire to escape. He agreed to help me and one night we ran away together. Later, in Kashi he introduced me to his family as his wife, and we began living together as husband and wife. Shivram was born two years thereafter. When Shivram was five years old, the music teacher suddenly succumbed to an asthma attack and passed away. After his, my husband's death, his family decided to tonsure me, as part of his funerary rituals. Though I resisted, no one paid any heed. They insisted that I had to be tonsured first, before they could take my husband's corpse away for cremation. They started quoting the scriptures at me, saying that unless my hair was burned along with his corpse, his soul would wander without release.

'Each drop of water from my hair that fell on the ground would amount to the years his soul would have to spend wandering in misery. They threatened, cajoled, and forced me to undergo tonsure. The torture did not stop there either. They also forced me to live like a widow. They fed me only once a day and only small, horribly inadequate amounts of limited food.

'My son was neglected too. No one gave him

any clothes, or bed coverings. His hands and feet would freeze during winters. Nobody cared about our medical needs either. If my son fell ill, he just suffered till he was better. People in my husband's household started dominating me, taking away the things that I possessed, and forcing me to undergo religious fasts that I had never even heard of. They began cursing me, if they happened to see me in the morning, and even in the deepest of winters, I was forced to bathe in cold water at dawn. If I now give you all the details of their torture, it would side-track from the rest of my story. So, to cut a long story short, after spending some time suffering this relentless torture, I left with my son, bundling up whatever little I had. Arriving at the Manikarnika Ghat, I initially stayed at a *dharmashala*, a hostel for the poor for the first two or three days, before accompanying a family of the goldsmith caste back to Pune. They agreed to let me travel with them.

'Arriving in Pune, I took up rented rooms in Belbaug. Soon, I made acquaintance with a priest called Vishnu Puranik from Mumbai who was also living in Belbaug. He was single, and lived in the room next to mine. After he finished with his daytime Puranic recitations at the Vishnu temple, he would collect a few tonsured widows like me and lecture them about the Puranas in the evenings. Some of these widows stayed till late in the night and even visited his room to seek advice. Seeing them, I too frequented some of his sermons. Soon, stowing away his pearls of wisdom, Vishnu Puranik started pursuing me. It did not take me long to understand his overtures.

'We decided to organize goddess rituals to dupe others, and he taught me some appropriate and useful incantations that I should say during the rituals. He would dress me up as Goddess Kali and organize a grand ritual every day. It was he who brought me that wig. Donning it, and the goddess's ornaments and finery, the worship session would commence in his room, and was attended by the public. Now, Goddess Kali had to be propitiated with meat and alcohol offerings. So, I ate my fill through these Kali rituals, while he pocketed the money. Sometimes, Puranik would also bring me alcohol and egg preparations from the market.

'Our business was going quite well, till one day a big religious conference was organized at Belbaug, attended by many influential critics and scholars. They heatedly discussed the case of a widow from the Shenoy caste, who was six months pregnant after having an affair with the family cook. Another widow from the high caste of goldsmiths had refused tonsure, and was having an affair with a stableboy. Hearing them fighting, wrangling, and shouting all day, I started feeling afraid. What would happen, when they, perhaps quite soon, found out about me? That would land me into terrible problems, and I would be forced to pay these Brahmins whatever little I had.

'Filled with terror, I fled Pune and arrived in Pandharpur. Here, I initially rented rooms with a temple priest, but I had to leave after there was a robbery in his house. Though only a few of his utensils were stolen, everything I had—my bundle and little trunk were gone. I lost all I had overnight. Though I initially cried and shouted, and then fasted, it was to no avail. Once inside the tiger's mouth, does the morsel ever return? I gradually abandoned all hope. Because of my worry about feeding myself and my son, the temple priest got me a job as a cook in another priest's house. As payment for my cooking, that priest conducted my son's *upanayana* ceremony. He has now promised to get my son married off when the time comes.'

8

Those Reformed

Though the story was long-drawn, Vinayak-*rao* listened attentively and did not interrupt. But he naturally wanted to understand how the landlady had ended up in her present state. It wasn't clear as yet who she was visiting every night.

So, he asked her point blank: 'Where do you go every evening? From where do you return every morning, like you did today?'

She answered: 'Since I have not hidden my past, it is useless now to hide my present. I am the temple priest's nephew's mistress—the priest for whom I cook. His nephew's wife died two years ago, and when I began staying with him openly, people started gossiping. So, he got me this house here, outside town. In the night, I go to the Vithoba temple and we meet there in an adjoining room.'

Vinayak-*rao* asked: 'Is this nephew also a priest at the Vithoba temple?'

She replied: 'Yes, most priests in town are linked to the Vithoba temple, and thousands of widows depend on the favours of temple priests over here—as their secret mistresses.'

Vinayak-*rao*: 'Do you want to continue your life as the mistress of a temple priest?'

Lady: 'What else shall I do? Who will take care of me? Who will get my son married?'

Vinayak-*rao*: 'But this is a terrible sin! Don't you feel afraid of leading a sinful life?'

Lady: 'I have led a sinful life from the very beginning. What is left to be afraid of now? If someone had shown me the right path, or had married me and given me a home and family, why would I wilfully suffer?'

Beginning to weep, she continued: 'Who would believe that I was once the daughter of such a rich and cultured family? My family was so respected that none dared to raise their gaze from my parents' feet. And look at my sad state now! Even after I was married, I was respected. But God lessened the years of my husband's life. I ran away from home only because Brahmins disallow widows from remarrying, and since then I have only been suffering countless sorrows. *Dada*, I have lived my life between the frying pan and the fire, and now, I only live to see my son growing up.'

Vinayak-*rao*: 'But you must leave this immoral path immediately!'

Lady: 'But then, how do I survive? If someone, despite my pathetic poverty and helplessness, were to include me in their family, and promise to get my son married, I would happily grow my hair and marry him. If you know of someone who is prepared to do this, then let me know. I will leave this immoral path immediately.'

Vinayak-*rao*: 'As far as our reformed younger generation is concerned, I have not come across anyone as yet who is brave enough to take the step of marrying a widow.'

Lady: 'Then, what is the use of this empty talk? Who would initiate a marriage in which the fire altar sets them on fire! Since no one comes forward to release us miserable widows from our fate, we must look for our own means to survive.'

Vinayak-*rao*: 'But this is a sinful path! You will have to suffer its consequences—the wrath of God.'

Lady: 'The wrath of God, is it? If God were indeed planning to mete out punishments, then before He punishes us poor widows, He would first have to punish those Brahmins and priests who exploit us. More than that, He would first have to punish you sanctimonious reformers! If you refuse to take the initiative, marry widows, and include us in your path of reform, then who can be held responsible for our immorality, the suffering and indignity forced upon us? It is you who will suffer the consequence of our turmoil, and it is you who are responsible for the abject condition of our children. How do you justify yourself—eating the food we cook? Seeing our suffering, abjection, and humiliation with your own eyes, how is it that you can keep eating morsel after morsel, without any moral compunction? And now adding insult to injury, you dare to lecture me about God's will, and threaten me with God's punishment? Let God punish us widows then! But first, He will certainly punish you. In which way, may I ask, have you ever personally helped widows?'

'I remember my life in Pune, making lamp wicks at the temple every evening and listening to people like you expound—those of you who are considered reformed. They would come and read aloud their opinions and letters that expressed commiseration for widows, for our suffering, for this and that—all big words. I have listened to plenty of letters written by you famous reformers, people like Lokahitavadi. I still remember his name. Listening to him, I would briefly feel that there was light at the other end of the tunnel for us widows—perhaps a better future ahead, since the government had allowed him to print his opinions after all. But many years have elapsed now, and no one has taken the initiative to implement these reforms. What on earth should we do? I ask now, where is this Mr. Lokahitavadi hiding? Why does he not lead a *Brahman Sabha* himself, a conference of Brahmins that will decide and argue on our behalf? Where is he? Wearing bangles and hiding near the stove somewhere with his cooking? The only thing he ever did was to spend money on the ink he used to write grandiose letters. If one does not act on one's promises, then how will empty words help to better the condition of us widows?'

Hearing her outburst, Vinayak-*rao* fell silent. He could not bring himself to say another word. He was convinced that, though the lady was leading an immoral life and kept immoral company, she had also gained enough awareness and discernment about her own condition due to all those reformed Brahmins of Pune, whose views she had heard. She felt bad about her life, but was also helpless to change it. The opinions, arguments, and newspaper articles written by reformers had shed light on her state, and had made her aware of its problems. But since that light lacked heat and energy, it was inadequate and unable to help her change her situation. The superficial strength of that light had instead hardened her against it, because that light had only helped to increase her suffering.

9

Released

It had grown late by then, and the lady had to attend to her cooking and other household chores. But, afterwards, at night, the couple began discussing all that the lady had shared.

Vinayak-*rao* said: 'I felt bad, hearing her miserable tale. This immorality has besieged women in our society for thousands of years, ruining the lives of so many widows.'

His wife replied: 'There is no doubt that countless lives have been wasted. But what is the use of regretting the past now? After all, are there any less widows in our own present times, who continue to suffer from this misery and immorality?'

Vinayak-*rao* said: 'Yes, my dear, you are right. In our world, one evil immorality hides inside the stomach of another, making a chain that is upheld by the structure of society itself. One evildoer finds another criminal, and a further link is created in that chain that steadily leads downwards into a deep abyss. No one ever climbs out of that abyss and back into the light again. The kind of company our landlady has been forced to keep at every life juncture has only led to her becoming ever lowered into that abyss.'

Yamuna: 'But there is still a silver lining. Our landlady has not turned away from the hope of climbing out of that abyss. She has not become afraid of a life that could lead her towards betterment. Don't lose hope in her. We will pray for her.'

Vinayak-*rao*: 'We need to carefully consider what we can do to release her from this dreadful trap. And we must also simultaneously return to debates about widow-remarriage. Widow-remarriage is vital for eliminating the immoral, exploitative practices of prostitution that moreover has domestic maidservants acting as pimps.'

Yamuna: 'Yes, instituting widow-remarriage is extremely vital. I wonder about all those people today who consider themselves to be of the higher class, but invite prostitutes and dancing girls into their homes to perform in their very own parlours. Don't such men have daughters, sisters, or daughters-in-law at home? If they were to ever give dignity to women in their family, then how could they encourage prostitution?'

Vinayak-*rao*: 'Once this patronage is halted,

prostitutes and pimps would lose their business, and then, the kidnapping and abducting of women to fuel this profession would also stop.'

Yamuna: 'And these holy pilgrimage towns. How unspeakably impure are these places!'

Vinayak-*rao*: 'Hindustan is full of such corrupt places. Whether it be pilgrimage towns like Nasik, Kashi, Kolhapur, Jejuri, Pandharpur, Tuljapur, Dwarka, and many thousands of others, priests always cheat the poor, simple-minded, and uneducated. Such places of unabated moral corruption and inauspiciousness are unthinkable in ordinary villages. These pilgrimage towns are dark caverns of sin. They masquerade as pious and pure, but only to hide the lies lurking underneath.'

Yamuna: 'What will you say to our landlady tomorrow? Did you notice how she turned the tables on you when you castigated her? But then, on the other hand, her argument is hardly to be faulted. If reformed men like you don't take the initiative and break these social evils that torture poor women, then to whom should they turn?'

Vinayak-*rao*: 'Our brains at this time can only function to a certain extent. Let us take rest now for we have grown exhausted with today's revelations. I am still shocked, and don't know what I will say to our landlady tomorrow. May God give us the wisdom to take the right decision in difficult times, and may he show us the righteous path ahead so that we can show this path to others.'

Both Vinayak-*rao* and Yamuna said their prayers and went to sleep. The next morning, Vinayak-*rao* asked the landlady to join them. He asked her whether she would cook for them, in return for shelter, food, clothing, and a safe life in their family. He promised to get her son educated and enable the boy to become independent and earn his living first, before getting him married. If the boy married too soon, that would only increase his poverty. While it was understandable that widows worried about their children's marriages, getting children married too soon was a mistake. The money so painstakingly collected despite extreme poverty was only wasted on wedding celebrations. No one cared for the child's education, moral development, or professional growth. If only all parental responsibilities ended with getting one's child married! If instead, one were realistic, one would realize that getting one's child married in haste, without caring for his education and independence first, would simply condemn the child to a vicious cycle in future that would regenerate his never-ending poverty.'

Vinayak-*rao* said: '*Bai*, I agree that widows like you have suffered terribly, and I am very sorry about it. I don't have the power to fulfil all your wishes, but I can help you financially, and assist you to turn away forever from this immoral path. I would like to help you, but the choice of accepting my help remains with you. If you really wish to change your life, you may accompany us.'

Hearing this, the widow became thoughtful first, and then immediately accepted the offer, deciding to join Vinayak-*rao* and Yamuna-*bai* along with her son, Shivram. Her decision made Vinayak-*rao* very happy. The couple settled her debts, and seeing that she would need another week to pack all her belongings, Vinayak-*rao* and Yamuna set out ahead to Satara, their next halt, asking the landlady to later join them there. Vinayak-*rao* left one of his servants behind in Pandharpur to accompany her.

10

The Brahmin Widow

Leaving Pandharpur behind, Vinayak-*rao* and Yamuna-*bai* reached a small village at dawn. As the bullocks rested at a stream, the carefree couple strolled around beholding the beauty of the eastern sky, lit up in a hundred different, vibrant colours just as the sun crept over the horizon.

Yamuna-*bai* commented: 'What a wonderfully refreshing cool breeze!'

Vinayak-*rao* answered: 'Look at the eastern sky! Doesn't it look as though it has been painted in brilliant gold? But can a paintbrush and human hand ever capture this dazzling brilliance? So many great emperors of yore have spent lakhs to have this brilliance painted on their palace walls, but their artificial pictures pale in comparison to the real sunrise.'

Yamuna-*bai*: 'There are so many different colours here. I can see scarlet, yellow, violet, *kirmiji*, and a myriad vivid other colours penetrating through the sun's golden rays. It was as though a goldsmith had poured molten gold all over the sky. How great is the beauty and genius of God! He has created so many miracles that fill us humans with wonder. I realize anew the meaning of the Christian scripture, "the sky demonstrates to us the grandeur of God." Also, how beautiful is the analogy of the bridegroom for the sun at dawn! The scripture says, "see the sun that emerges like a bridegroom from his room."'

Vinayak-*rao* said: 'Look at all those little birds that have just awakened! Listen to their melodious singing. Hear the sweet chirping of their little ones. See, over there! A small bird emerges from its nest and solemnly looks around, as if contemplating where it will search for food.'

Yamuna-*bai*: 'Do birds even think?'

Vinayak-*rao*: 'No, my dear, birds don't think! God has given them an innate nature and instinct, a bodily wisdom according to which they unthinkingly act. Unlike us, they cannot discern good from bad. They are never dissatisfied and never bored. That is why they are always happy.'

Yamuna-*bai*: 'Only if we humans could live that way—in an uncomplicated manner. Being happy like birds and being satisfied with what God has given us! If only if we could rid ourselves of jealousy, hatred, and envy for the things others have. If birds could be satisfied with what they have, then why can't we? We are so foolish—madly involved in our worldly pursuits, aspiring to acquire things we don't need—things that are, in any case, impossible to own, desiring to rule the whole world as if it were our fiefdom. God teaches us the correct way to live our lives through the bird.'

Vinayak-*rao*: 'Listening to you, I am reminded of a great preacher who once said, "don't worry about what to eat; and don't worry about what to wear! Look at the birds in the sky! Neither do they sow seeds, neither do they harvest crops. They don't store grains in warehouses because God in heaven gives them enough to eat." Now, aren't we wiser than birds? Then why can't we realize this simple truth?'

Yamuna-*bai*: 'Yes, I was thinking the same. Though foolish and lazy people interpret this to mean that they don't need to work, this is not what the dictum means. It means that though we should work for our livelihoods, earn, and buy our necessities, we should not be preoccupied, obsessed, and perennially worried about it. The mind must be free, healthy, and capable of higher tasks. It is these higher tasks that God demands from us.'

Vinayak-*rao*: 'All God's actions are good and beautiful. And all His actions contain divine teachings.

He has created us human beings in His own image—good and beautiful! Humans, being created thus, were originally wise, pure, and just. But then, they began having selfish thoughts, doubts, and suspicions, and it is only because of this that they plunged themselves into misery.'

Yamuna-*bai*: 'I am forever reminded of our poor, widowed landlady in Pandharpur. She was as innocent, trusting, and pure as that bird. If she had remained on the moral path, she would have enjoyed great happiness. What a tragedy! She was first separated from her family, and then, even after she tried to live happily with her husband's family, her happiness did not last. She became snared in the noose of cruel hunters, who pitted her into suffering and cast her upon an unrighteous path. I am glad God has put her into our hands. I hope and pray we can help and protect her and her son.'

The couple talking thus, strolled here and there in the fresh morning air of the countryside, till their cart driver called out: '*Bai*! Let us be off! It is late already, and there is still a long journey ahead. If we tarry now, the bullocks will tire easily in the mid-morning heat.'

He yoked the bullocks and seating his master and mistress in the cart, egged his bullocks on to such good speed that they reached the next village by afternoon. Vinayak-*rao* halted the cart at the village headman's house with a plan to rest till the afternoon heat subsided. They would resume thereafter and halt for the night in the next village. The servants procured food and wood for their afternoon meal and soon had a blazing fire going.

Just then, a Brahmin widow, brass pot in hand, came by and stood in front of the headman's door, crying out plaintively: '*Rama Krishnaya Namah* (obeisance to the Gods Rama and Krishna). Please, *bai*, give me some alms. It is one in the afternoon and there is not one morsel of food in my belly! Oh, Rama!'

As Yamuna-*bai* peered out from behind the curtains, she saw the Brahmin widow chance upon the servants cooking their afternoon meal.

Looking at the wood fire longingly, she beseeched one of them: '*Dada*, could you please lend me a piece of wood? I am a poor widow and I only have some rice that I received as alms. If you give me a piece of your firewood, I will cook and eat the rice and bless you for your kindness. To donate to cows and to Brahmins is a deed of merit that is never lost. May the Gods of Kashi Rameshwar shower their blessings on you.'

Hearing her entreaties, Rav-*ji* (Vinayak-*rao*'s servant), who was sitting next to the fire kneading dough, threw her a piece of wood.

The Brahmin Widow

At this, the Brahmin widow said: '*Dada*, how can I take this wood that is sullied by your touch as you cook? We are Brahmins. This piece of wood must be unsullied if a Brahmin widow like me has to cook on it. Will you please allow me to pick a piece of wood for myself, with my own hands?'

As the widow haltingly made her way towards the wood pile, another one of Vinayak-*rao*'s servants, who was feeding the bullocks shouted out: 'Get out, you dirty, useless creature! You tonsured Brahmin drudges are spread all across the country like a pestilence of stray dogs. You won't get anything here. Be off with you!'

Calling out to Rav-*ji*, he reiterated: 'Don't, Rav-*ba*; don't give her anything.'

Rav-*ji*: 'Oh, let her take what she wants. She is only a widow. What will we lose if she takes a piece of wood?'

At this the other servant answered: 'It's not that I grudge anyone a piece of wood! The poor should definitely be helped. But arrogant women like these hypocrite Brahmin widows roaming the countryside, begging at villages and pretending to be pure should be condemned. They fornicate with whomever comes their way in secret and become pregnant and in the daylight hours, they look down their noses at non-Brahmin castes like Sonars, Shimpis, and Kunbis. In front of the world, they make this great drama of purity! But inside they are something else! Once a widow like this one, bathing near where my wife was washing her clothes in the river, picked a huge fight and accused my wife of deliberately splashing dirty water on her and destroying her purity. In reality, not a single drop had fallen on her. It was just a huge show in which she publicly abused and humiliated my wife. Later it was revealed that this widow's own sister—another widow herself, had become pregnant! After this was reported, the police kept the sister under house arrest lest she kill the child, and that house was in our own locality. This is the real truth of this plague of tonsured widows!'

Hearing this, the Brahmin widow said: 'Cartman *Dada*, I am not like those other widows. Maybe some widows are immoral, but how can you think that we are all that the same? Why would I otherwise come here begging? My brothers-in-law drove me out of the house and it is my fate now to listen to your cruel words. There was a time I fed and clothed others and now, this is my fate! Whatever can be done?'

Hearing this, Yamuna-*bai* came out of the house and scolded the cartman for his harsh words. Then turning to the Brahmin widow, she asked: '*Bai*, where do you come from? Where is your village?'

Brahmin widow: '*Bai*, I was only begging for

The Brahmin Widow

some wood from your servant when this other man began shouting and abusing me.'

Yamuna-*bai*: 'Yes, I heard him and I have just scolded him. But now, I am asking you, where are you from?'

Brahmin widow: '*Bai*, I am originally from Bijapur, but I roam these regions nowadays, begging for alms.'

Yamuna-*bai*: 'Don't you have your own family in Bijapur?'

Brahmin widow: '*Bai*, I once had a large family. And even now, my brothers-in-law and their wives continue to stay in Bijapur.'

Yamuna-*bai*: 'Then, why do you roam around here, asking for alms?'

Brahmin widow: '*Bai*, what is the use of telling you my story! When my husband was at his deathbed, he made a will leaving me the house, a part of the farm, and its produce. My brothers-in-law snatched away these papers and made a court case against me. They won the case because no one supported me. All the court officials and lawyers asked for bribes. I begged them to support me, promising them money if I won. I even sold off my remaining jewellery to pay them. But still, they did not let me win. I went to the court every day and also sat outside the court peon's house every single day, but no one helped me. My brothers-in-law bribed the court officials and made them promise to defeat me. They tore up and threw away all my applications and after I lost the case, my brothers-in-law threw me out of the house. Now I am a beggar, roaming the streets.'

Yamuna-*bai*: 'Wouldn't it have been ideal for you to remarry? Then you would have been spared all this.'

Brahmin widow: '*Bai*, how can you even think this? We are Brahmins. Are we like widows from the Kunbi or Mali castes? Those widows are Shudra. They don't have a religion! We, who follow the Brahmin religion can never even think of doing this.'

Yamuna-*bai*: 'Yes, but times have changed. Now, people are reconsidering widow-remarriage.'

Brahmin widow: 'Yes, that is the tragedy of our times. And this is the true nature of British oppression that has corrupted the life of Brahmins. Now they are after widows! *Bai*, our religion, and its purity has come under threat. The defenders of cows—Brahmins—have lost their power. Now, anyone can do whatever they like. I would say, at least we Brahmin widows must keep to our religion and resist becoming polluted. If we can't fill our stomachs, we can at least ask for alms. Food received as alms is of the purest nature; there is nothing purer than it. The amount one gets is enough to fill one's stomach. We widows can go on pilgrimage and it accords us merit and releases us from our past deeds. But pilgrimage is also a matter

The Brahmin Widow

of luck. Not everyone can manage it. But yes, one should go to temples like Kashi Vishweshwar, to Gaya and to Prayag and other places. This birth is nothing! One should pray that the human soul be released from rebirth and attain liberation.'

Yamuna-*bai* was taken aback at the widow's unexpected lecture on Brahminism. Curious to know more, she provocatively asked: 'But *bai*, isn't it also because Brahmins disallow widows from remarrying that immorality in society also increases? Didn't you hear what our cartman just said? Also, doesn't asking for alms burden others? Begging makes a person lazy and good for nothing. This is why it is better for widows to remarry.'

Brahmin widow: '*Bai*, which caste do you belong to? Though you look like a Brahmin, you say preposterous things! It is actually that dratted *kumpini* that has abolished sati. Abolishing sati is directly responsible for the rising immorality of widows. In earlier times, widows went to their husbands' pyres and that controlled their licentiousness. In fact, they left behind legacies of honour. Now that sati is disallowed, widows forced to remain alive, hoist the flag of immorality wherever they go. You tell me, what is better? People have stopped donating to Brahmins, and the earth is therefore angry and has stopped yielding grain, and instead generates droughts.

Also, that *kumpini* is ruled by a woman, so she does not see the need to punish immorality among women. As a result, these widows have all the freedom in the world. If this were earlier *Peshwai* times, these women would have been punished—made to stand on burning hot frying pans, I tell you. Now, the good old times are over and people do whatever they want!'

Yamuna-*bai*: 'But still, I cannot condone begging. I consider it lowly to beg. Begging cannot be justified as religion.'

Brahmin widow: 'You are speaking as if I have personally invented the practice of begging for alms. It is not I alone who praises its virtues. The great sages of yore have also praised it, describing the seeking of alms as an honourable deed.'

Yamuna-*bai*: 'Do you mean that the sages have actually prescribed begging?'

Brahmin widow: 'Indeed! I can recite to you some verses from the famous religious text *Dasbodh*, composed by none other than Ramdas Swami.'

Yamuna-*bai*: 'So, it seems you can read!'

Brahmin widow: 'Not at all! I spent six months as a cook at a priest's residence and learned some of these verses by heart there as I heard them being recited every day.'

Yamuna-*bai*: 'Fine! Then recite to me those few lines that you know. Let's see what *Baba* Ramdas has to say about begging.'

The Brahmin widow began singing the verses out loud:

The main task of a Brahmin monk is to learn to ask for alms. His task is to protect the purity of alms, for it is only a monk who can truly eat till he is fulfilled. Separating themselves from the householder's world, saints who ask for alms discover the nectar of life and the pleasure of elixir, even as they desist from the luxuries of the body. He who asks for alms learns the glory of God and all those monks who ask for alms, demonstrate their lack of desire. The Brahmin who allocates his meals to fixed homes every day, relinquishes his independence. He arranges his food in fixed households and soon his life becomes monotonous, depriving him of new experience and spiritual growth. Move away to new places every day! Travel to distant lands! And subsist on alms without embarrassment.

Asking for alms is honourable indeed! A monk is never a stranger, for when he survives on alms without embarrassment, every country where he goes becomes like his own home. Stop feeling shy or hesitant. Don't avoid asking for alms. For, the miracles of a life spent on alms can be enjoyed by the young and old alike, helping them to realize God. The alms one receives is Kamdhenu, the cow of wish fulfilment, and the person who disregards alms is unfortunate indeed! Alms introduce a monk to new people and they save him toil, as small amounts can easily be spared for everyone. Alms induce a state of fearlessness, of spiritual greatness and independence, that introduces the monk to God. There can be no obstacle for the monk who is free to spend his time fruitfully. The monk who asks for alms without embarrassment is immortal. Alms are a boon in odd hours. A fasting person never dies, for he is never a burden on others. He always finds someone who feeds him.

Asking for alms is better than working, tending to animals, shops, or farms, since it is honourable. There is no greater renunciation than alms and no greater fortune than renunciation. He who denies renunciation, denies his own fortune. A monk is happy with small things and takes only a fistful even when offered a heap. To ask for alms and to renounce is safety. Speak gently that it should give peace and happiness to the heart. Speak humbly and little, for the asking for alms frees the monk forever!

Finishing her recitation, the Brahmin widow said to Yamuna-*bai*: 'Now, I am really hungry. Can you give me some pulses? I will eat it with rice. I have been eating dry rice with salt for the last four days. The stomach and its hunger harass even the most dutiful. Now, it is two in the afternoon. To which market shall I go? And who will give me alms over there at this time of the afternoon? Oh God!'

Yamuna-*bai* took pity on the Brahmin widow and gave her all the grains she required. Still, the widow asked for some money as *dakshina*, so that the ritual of giving alms to a Brahmin widow would be completed. This, the widow said, would accord Yamuna-*bai* as the donor, the merit of worshipping at the temples of Kashi Vishweshwar.

Hearing this, Yamuna-*bai* said: 'I have not given you food and money out of a desire to gain merit! It is my duty as a human being to feed another who is hungry. This does not make me a great person. But if I had sent you away at this hour without giving you any food, I would have certainly been a sinner. But please don't consider me as one of those women from whom you regularly elicit charity and also don't ever think that I consider giving alms a godly deed. It is only in the glory of God that I gave you this grain. Now, take it.'

Brahmin widow: 'Whatever you say, *bai*. All said and done, you have fed me my daytime meal today. May God bless you.'

Saying this, she left. Meanwhile, Vinayak-*rao* had been listening to the entire conversation from inside. After the Brahmin widow left, he said: 'So, you won quite the battle today. See what kind of people one meets in life—each more stubborn than the next! It becomes almost impossible to defend one's opinion unless one fights a battle.'

Hearing this, Yamuna-*bai* said: 'I have never met a widow like her in my life. I thought all widows wanted to remarry.'

Vinayak-*rao*: 'Oh no, don't make that mistake, my dear! Even if the majority want to remarry, there are others who get angry even if the word "widow-remarriage" is whispered. And it is difficult to convince them. These widows prefer to suffer and tolerate exploitation but they strongly resist any improvements made to their condition. These are conservative women, who believe in and are fond of archaic superstitions. According to them, it is a bad thing that the government has abolished sati. That the government will soon abolish the drowning of infant girl children and stop widows from committing suicide is also considered bad by them.'

As they talked thus, their hostess having finished cooking, invited them to lunch. As they entered the small inside room, they found two plates neatly arranged next to each other. The couple exclaimed appreciatively at the cosy, clean, and beautiful room. Its doors were made of the stout, rough wood of the jackfruit tree and the floor was polished and smeared clean with cow dung. Rays of sunlight creeping in through the thatched roof were reflected on the ground like small, shining, round gold coins with atoms of sunshine dancing in those sunrays. The room was well lit and the walls were smeared with red-brown umber. There was a small loft of rough beams above them that had bundles of leaf plates stacked together.

The Brahmin Widow

There was an air of tidy domesticity everywhere. A large mortar lay in one corner; the oblique rays of sunlight on its pestle leaning against the wall made it gleam like silver. The other side of the room had neatly folded rugs piled on top of each other. Despite all that was stored there, the room was well-kept and looked beautiful rather than untidy. As the couple admired the room, their hostess heaped their plates with aubergines, okra, rice, and lentil curry topped with dollops of golden, clarified butter. The butter was so rich that its heady aroma filled the room. Offering them cups of rich butter milk, their hostess said: 'I hope you enjoy your meal! It is unfortunately the only kind of food we can offer you here in rural, humble homes like ours. We don't have all the cooking ingredients available in the city. Please accept our humble fair. Yamuna-*bai*, if you prefer fresh yogurt instead of butter milk, I have some kept aside.'

Yamuna-*bai* said: 'Oh, we need nothing more, *bai*! The food is delicious, and it tastes better than the food in the city. The okra is tender and tasteful and the clarified butter is unparalleled. *Bai*, I am very fond of village life. The quality of air over here is so pure and uncontaminated. The farms and orchards are so green and shaded. The birds sing in such sweet voices! Everything is refreshing and different.'

They ate their fill in this manner and rested awhile

till the afternoon heat subsided. Their servants Rav-*ji* and Govinda also rested, as did their animals, who ate their fodder and drank enough water to last them the journey ahead. Soon, Govinda called to Rav-*ji*, saying: 'Wake up Rav-*ji*! It is evening. We need to reach our next destination by nightfall. Call the master and mistress. If it gets too dark, the path ahead will become too difficult to see.'

Hearing this, Vinayak-*rao* and Yamuna-*bai* also immediately prepared to leave, and climbing onto their cart pulled by the two loyal bullocks (called Moti and Paula), the party set off speedily, reaching Satara by nightfall.

11

The Conference

As soon as they reached Satara, Vinayak-*rao* received a long letter from his friend that contained descriptions of the pathetic state of widows. Being saddened by this, Vinayak-*rao* read the letter aloud to his wife.

After hearing him out, she said: 'Today our host has organized a celebration to mark the birth of his son. Many educated, honourable gentlemen from the town are invited to visit in the evening. Why not read them out this letter, and elicit their response about widow-remarriage? Maybe our great, educated guests this evening will agree, and maybe the practice of widow remarriage will gradually begin, at least in Satara.'

The home where Vinayak-*rao* and Yamuna-*bai* had arrived belonged to the head clerk of the Satara commissioner, a position of great authority referred to as Sir Karkoon. Their host, this head clerk, was of the Sonar caste and had been nominated for this position from Mumbai. He and Vinayak-*rao* had been classmates in Mumbai. This was the reason why Vinayak-*rao* had come to stay with him as a guest. But it was equally obvious that the two men diverged in their opinions about reform. While Jagannath-*ji*, Vinayak-*rao*'s Sonar friend, was interested in reform during his student days, this interest had only been a strategic pretence. It had been necessary for him to claim this interest, for it had helped him to write essays and participate in elocution competitions on the subject as part of his schoolwork. Therefore, though he engaged with reform, he did not really have any feeling for it. His own arguments did not penetrate his heart. Once he returned home, he would leave reformist discussions behind and busy himself with entertainment. In his free time, he would bet on horses, accompany his father to meetings with famous and influential people, and attended feasts, musical soirees, theatres, dances, and *tamasha* performances. He strolled in various gardens, played chess, and entertained influential visitors, impressing them with his learning.

Following his father's advice to keep his engagement with reform limited to schoolbooks, he focused only on learning good English and good arithmetic. This was also the direction his father encouraged him to take—English, arithmetic, and the strategic pretence of reform that would secure him a scholarship. His father advised Jagannath to focus on securing a scholarship, after which he planned to place his son in an influential position. He was aware of what it entailed to be a person of high social status and he knew that his son would need to interact with many important people. Besides, his son would require financial support from businessmen and commercial magnates and so, they too would have to be appeased. Criticism could harm his son, especially in his important and formative years.

While younger boys from similar castes—many among them Sonars, liked to call themselves reformers, claiming that they wanted to improve society, Jagannath's father was worried that these boys would negatively influence his impressionable son who would then be swayed away from self-interest. Hence, his son would have to be controlled and taught to say 'yes' only to his teachers. At the same time, he would have to internally desist from imbibing this learning. This learning that was considered harmful by Jagannath's father, was thus fit to be immediately discarded. Those who wanted to imbibe it could go ahead, but his son would certainly not have anything to do with it. And in any case, school and school friends hardly lasted for one's lifetime.

Jagannath's father wanted his son to interact superficially with his classmates, till a time his interests were served and not allow their discussions to penetrate any deeper. Once Jagannath left school no one would care about what he thought and why he thought so. Young boys nowadays were rebellious. They broke caste strictures; stopped going to the temple; stopped respecting their elders, Brahmins, and priests. He did not want his son to become like those boys. He wanted his son to snub widow-remarriage advocates, and stop the charade of reform altogether now that he had a job. That would only invite stigma and ill-repute to good families like theirs. Whenever anyone asked why he opposed widow-remarriage, Jagannath should answer by asking him in return to first get his own tonsured mother remarried first.

Jagannath regularly received such advice from his father. And because of this, the tender shoots inspired by higher education were burned in the harsh light of an overbearing sun. Jagannath avoided all meetings where reform and widow-remarriage was discussed. He only attended when important people were invited, for example, at a prize distribution ceremony in the town hall, or at a festive gathering to honour an important person. Those were places where Jagannath-*ji* readily accompanied his father and sat next to important people. He would attend

The Conference

government functions and make himself noticeable by making conspicuously large charitable donations. If he came across an Englishman with sympathy for reformers, he would nod and agree like his father had taught him to do.

At the time he was studying in Mumbai, Jagannath had written some letters to the editor in a famous English newspaper of that time, criticising widow-remarriage. Though he could not openly oppose it since he knew the government's opinion on the topic, he overstretched himself in trying to prove that widows did not suffer in any special way, apart from missing and grieving for their dead husbands. By writing in this way, he also curried favour with those who were influential enough to get him the important job of a head clerk at the Satara commissioner's office. Once he arrived in Satara, he flattered all the Brahmins working in high positions there to gain their favour. Jagannath had become a selfish hypocrite. Vinayak-*rao* knew all this and was not too hopeful that Jagannath and the type of friends he kept—the ultra-Brahmin variety—would take too well to a discussion on widow-remarriage. And why would they listen to his arguments? Yet, truth hardly dies an easy death and keeping faith in God, Vinayak-*rao* took up the thoughtful suggestion made by his wife and decided to bring up the topic of widow-remarriage for discussion that evening.

A band of musicians was already playing when the Brahmin guests for the evening arrived. They hailed from all over town and decked in their finery, began seating themselves in Jagannath's front hall. They were followed by civil servants, government employees working in high positions, and influential lawyers. Jagannath performed the appropriate rituals for commemorating the birth of a male child and distributed cut pieces of fresh coconut, sweets, betel leaf, and flowers among guests. He sprinkled them with perfumed rose water and everyone's mood lifted as the evening progressed. Shamelessly, Jagannath had also invited a courtesan for the evening soiree, who was to perform a dance; and this, despite Vinayak-*rao*'s objections. However, this courtesan was unable to attend since her younger sister had died of cholera that very morning.

Not only could she not attend, but because her status was so high in Satara, none of the other courtesans of Satara dared to attend either, not daring to break their solidarity with her. So, in one sense, Vinayak-*rao* was pleased that his objections had been coincidentally upheld and he attended the evening celebrations in a somewhat calmer state of mind.

After the ceremony, the Brahmin scholar Moro-*shastri* offered his snuffbox to Krishna-*shastri* and to Ragho-*pant* sitting next to him and said: 'There is no other achievement greater than begetting a son.'

Krishna-*shastri* immediately quoted a few Sanskrit verses extolling the virtues of begetting a son and playfully gesturing to Vishwambhar-*bhatji*, another esteemed Brahmin, asked: 'Now, what kind of comment would you like to make on this?'

At this, Vishwambhar-*bhatji* excitedly inhaled a pinch of snuff, wiped his nose with the end of his *dhoti*, threw back his head and squeezed his eyes shut, as if trying to remember. Then jerking his head, he recited another Sanskrit stanza to match the one quoted by Krishna-*shastri*.

When Ragho-*pant*, not understanding these Sanskrit verses asked for an explanation, Moro-*shastri* explained: 'These verses mean, "It is through the birth of a son that a man achieves victory. It is through the birth of a grandson that a man becomes immortal. And it is through the birth of a great grandson that a man achieves *adityaloka*, becoming akin to a deity himself. These are the benefits of having a son."'

As the knowledgeable Brahmin priests discussed this, monks began lining up for alms on the other side of the room. One of them, called Dhond-*bhatji*, said: 'This occasion of the birth of a son has been wonderfully celebrated by *Shetji* (referring to Jagannath-*ji*), by donating to and feeding us Brahmins. He is lucky to have so many Brahmins in his home today, who bless him. Nowadays, no one engages with religious tasks and the importance of Brahmins is lessening. Indeed! There are very few great, charitable persons like him.'

To this, another Brahmin guest called Mairal-*bhat* retorted: 'Indeed, yes! It is doubtless that this celebration of a son's birth has commenced wonderfully. The fame of our *yajman*'s achievements has spread everywhere like the fragrance of flowers and sandalwood. The *grihasta ashrama* of this young man is exemplary! He is supremely civilized and his wife is a pure lady. The couple are so righteous. Without the merit accrued from their past births, all this would have been impossible.'

Ram-*bhat* Joshi, sitting next to Mairal-*bhat* quoted a Sanskrit verse and then explained: 'That a man's domestic life is indeed blissful can be counted from the fact that his sons are always intelligent and his wife always sweet-tongued and adoring; that he earns good money and his servants are always obedient. He always welcomes and entertains guests at home, he is a devotee of Shiva, he keeps the company of sages and he eats sweetmeats at home; that man's domestic life is forever blessed.'

Ram-*bhat* was of the opinion that since Jagannath's life contained all these qualities, he was indeed a blessed man. The Brahmins praised and flattered Jagannath all evening and hearing them filled the latter with such boastful pride and self-importance that he could hardly contain himself.

Keshav-*rao* Daftardar, sitting next to Vinayak-*rao* said: 'Now, if *Shetji* had had a daughter instead of a son, there wouldn't have been such a grand celebration today. It is quite another achievement to have a son.'

Vinayak-*rao* answered: 'All children are a gift from God, whether they be sons or daughters. Whichever of the two God gives us, we should be grateful for both.'

Daftardar: 'Yes, you are not wrong, but the birth of a son is a separate matter compared to the birth of a daughter. A daughter is, after all, the source of all sorrows. A woman, however fine, is lowly and degraded. She cannot be auspicious.' Quoting a Sanskrit verse, he clarified: 'It is women's nature to lie, behave thoughtlessly, be devious, foolish, greedy, inauspicious, and cruel.'

Vinayak-*rao*: 'That is completely untrue! To consider women lowly and degraded is against the will of God. Women are hardly more sinful than men. In the beginning, God created both men and women as equally pure and talented, but they later became corrupted. Women are not specially to blame for this. In our country, women have been neglected; kept in abject and pathetic conditions wherein they lack basic education. And because of this, they are further blamed and accused of being lowly. If they had as much freedom and dignity as men, if they were to be equally educated, then they would hardly be considered lowly, degraded, and foolish.'

At this, Keshav-*rao* turned to Jagannath-*shet* and said: 'What do you think of what our friend over here says? Should women be given equal freedom to men? How would you answer him?'

Jagannath: 'He is right, but only to a limited extent. Nowadays, many reformers argue on behalf of women and even argue for their superiority over men. Young students everywhere, even in the smallest of schools, are busy writing essays and participating in heated debates and elocution competitions about women's emancipation and widow-remarriage. But these are just inexperienced students! What do they understand? They follow their schoolmasters and discourse precociously about things they hardly comprehend, when advocating for the demolishing of traditions in our country that have continued for thousands of years.'

Vinayak-*rao* said to Jagannath: 'If you argue this way, Jagannath-*ji*, then whom are we to turn to for future leadership? I am sure you have read a lot, but the difficulties faced by a widower is not even a thousandth of the sorrows and difficulties faced by widows!'

Jagannath-*ji* turned to Keshav-*rao* and said: 'You see? All their knowledge is derived from books. After the English came to India, they wrote hundreds of books on Hindu rituals, religious practices, and the traditions of India. On the other hand, they know very little about our domestic lives and social interactions. Things that are heard can be half false after all and the things they have written are in any case selectively based on descriptions provided by Hindu interlocutors who tell the English what they want to hear. The new generation of educated youth have been brought up on these half-baked English books. They champion these books since these form the basis of their own social status as educated and knowledgeable.'

Keshav-*rao*: 'Exactly! One must be loyal to one's salt.'

Vinayak-*rao*: 'This is nonsense! If only you had carried out your own research on the sorrowful condition of widows in India, you would have better appreciated the truth of my words.'

Jagannath: 'I don't feel that widows suffer as much as you say. What should anyone do if their husbands pass away? There are thousands of Englishwomen after all, who never marry. Their lives are hardly steeped in an ocean of sorrow! Similarly, widows are happy in our society. Their parents look after them lovingly, feed and clothe them, and allow them to travel on pilgrimages. They fast but only ritually, and busy themselves with religious activities like chanting, worship, and prayer. The only thing that perhaps plagues them is the sorrow of their husbands' death. It is a personal loss and a grief. But this is the way of the world. With time, they slowly emerge from this grief. Even a mother, who loses her only son emerges from her bereavement in three or four years. It is the same for widows. Many of them who are child widows don't even understand this loss, for they have no idea of what a husband is, and what marital relationships or pleasure can mean. So, they hardly miss their husbands and feel no grief. As far as old, widowed women are concerned, they don't have the slightest desire to remarry. Now, the only group that may be of concern here is young widows. But once they readjust to their new lives within parental homes, they busy themselves with household chores, and hardly find time after that to miss their husbands.'

Vinayak-*rao*: 'It seems as though you support the tonsuring of widows! Is it acceptable to you that after widowhood, women are uglified and humiliated, all their ornaments and finery confiscated'?

Jagannath: 'What is wrong with that? It is true, they look ugly at first, and feel awkward and embarrassed, but soon they get used to it. All this is only a matter of habit! The first two or three times, a widow feels

The Conference

embarrassed, sitting in front of a barber, but later she starts teaching him his job, asking him to shave as closely as possible. And how many of these widowed women are there really? Out of a total population of twenty crores in India, there are not more than two lakh widows. This is just a fistful of salt in the sea. What is the point of making such a commotion about widow-remarriage?'

Vinayak-*rao*: 'This perspective can be applied to all social problems, isn't it? Nothing will ever improve then! One can, for example, use the same argument about female infanticide in Kutch and Kathiawar. One could justify female infanticide by saying that it is hardly cruel for infants who die easily at the slightest pressure applied to their throats. Moreover, their mothers are used to doing this and not one drop of blood is spilt. In fact, their mothers are perhaps, saving them from a life exposed to illness, sorrows, and worries. Also, the parents are relieved as they don't have to struggle to bring up their daughters in poverty. One could justify it further by saying that since God decided where these girls would be born, their deaths too, are actually predestined by God and executed by their parents as sacred duty. Is that the implication of your argument? Are you also opposing the government for breaking this thousand-year-old, ancient, customary, traditional practice of female infanticide among Rajputs? The death of five hundred Rajput infants every year is after all little, compared to the entire number of infants born annually in India.'

Keshav-*rao*: 'It is impossible to understand these lofty arguments. I have heard the government is about a pass a widow-remarriage law. Now, how can that be beneficial? Won't there be utter chaos if widows begin remarrying?'

Jagannath: 'I don't like it that the government interferes with our traditional customs and abolishes Hindu widowhood practices. The government should stay away from religious matters. Now the government mandates that widows, irrespective of caste, are legally entitled to remarry. They will continue to own property and their children born from remarriage will be legitimate heirs.'

Keshav-*rao*: 'Right, right! Now, widows can do whatever they like. If they don't like their first husbands, they can also murder them and remarry. It has been foretold that one day, our law of the caste system preserved through the *varnasankara* will forever be demolished. We are living to see that day now. The English will not be content till they ruin us. They are interested in passing this law so that it disarms, weakens, and vanquishes the Hindu community. They want to convert us to their religion to eliminate our resistance to their government. This

The Conference

same method was also used by the Muslims in the time before the British. They converted everyone around them to Islam and through conversion, strengthened their own empire. The same thing happens now. The only difference is that the English tread gently and use strategic compromises whereas the Muslims used force. The English tread gently only so that we don't take on the Vishnu avatar of Narsimha and rise up against them. If that happens, we will surely vanquish them. If we were to attack with adequately vicious ferocity, they will lose against us. My little son at home often reads a story about the sun and the wind. The modus-operandi of the British is similar. Though the force of the wind could not blow away a blanket wrapped tightly around the shoulders of a man, the gentle but persistent rays of the hot sun were enough to inspire within him a desire to remove that blanket on his own. This is the only difference between the Muslims and the English. Even if there is no personal oppression under British rule and society seems happy enough under their reformist policies, the harm they do us is greater than that of the Muslims.'

Vinayak-*rao*, who had been patiently listening, answered Jagannath-*shetji* thus: 'It is doubtless that you have gained tremendous favour and support for your opinions. But it is also unfair to deny the truth just for the sake of gaining fame and favour. All of you have accused me of basing my support of widow-remarriage and my opinion that widows indeed live in abject neglect, on my English education and on English books. But this is completely untrue. I have been travelling through the country in these past few months, and have personally witnessed the suffering of widows. I have closely witnessed their horrifying privations, and I am completely convinced that they are from among the most unfortunate creatures in this world. Their condition is more calamitous than any other human being's state today. You have all also seen examples of this in your own life but have decided to shut your eyes to the sorrows of widows, because you don't want to see the bad in your society, and the corruption of your everyday lives. So, how can I make you think of things that you are deliberately avoiding? How will you ever see the extent of horror, exploitation, and suffering these women undergo? You say that widows don't really suffer and that widowhood does not create any social disturbance, but how can I argue with you if you do not want to see the chaos produced by widowhood? I can only tell you what I have seen, and what I have learned and witnessed, and not more than that! Perhaps if I read aloud from a letter I recently received from an associate, my words will finally convince you.'

12

Arjun and the Lady

As the conversation progressed, a Telang Brahmin sitting in a corner tuned his musical instrument, the *rudraveena,* and began playing it. He sang a few verses in a mixture of Sanskrit, Telugu, and Hindustani and the last two lines of his song were apt enough to remain strong in Vinayak-*rao*'s memory of that evening: 'When one gentleman meets another, it is like the union between camphor and a smouldering stick of sandalwood. But when an evil man meets another man as evil as himself, their union is like poison mixed with *bhang*.'

Another guest, Vishveshwar-*shastri*, who was earlier a student of an English school in Pune, said to Vinayak-*rao*: 'Please proceed with your letter.'

And Vinayak-*rao* began reading aloud:

Greetings! I received your letter from Pandharpur and was overwhelmed with your description of widows and their piteous condition. I am responding to your request by providing you with a description of widows over here. All my information is true and I present you with a real account of their difficulties.

A man known as Pant, an emissary of a big landowner from South India, recently shifted here to work for the British administration. He has a ten-year-old boy and an older daughter. The man is affluent, but his problem is this daughter, who became widowed at the age of twelve. He feels extremely sorry for her and though his mind is plagued with worry, he is unable to find a solution. Since Brahmins do not allow their widows to remarry, she is condemned to a lifelong of widowhood, living in her father's house till her end. Her mother tries and diverts her mind by prescribing her the worship of the *tulsi* plant, and by enjoining her to undertake ritual fasts.

She took her widowed daughter to the Maruti temple and to the Shiva temple to keep her busy with *kirtan* and chanting over there. But the girl continued to be unhappy and emotionally disturbed. Comparing herself to the married daughters and the daughters-in-law of other families, she felt ashamed of her own pathetic condition. As soon as she attained puberty, she was immediately tonsured. After that her fair skin and beautiful face looked ugly. Now, it so happened at this time that her younger brother joined the local Marathi school and in order that he may excel in his studies, the father engaged a local tutor who would come to the home to teach the boy. This tutor initially came every day, but soon left because the payment was low and irregular. However, since he knew the family well, he continued to visit their home informally.

Now, coincidentally at this time, the local administrative officer was touring the area on horseback and as he went around the region, he saw a strange, long object lying in the garbage pit outside the back door-lane of the Pant household. The crows had pounced upon it. Piqued, the officer had that object excavated and it turned out to be the corpse of a premature but beautiful five-month-old baby. The officer reported the matter to the police and recommended an in-depth investigation. First, the police apprehended all the widows from nearby households. But they could not identify the perpetrator. Then, they started investigating the Pant family. The girl's mother accepted that her daughter was a widow but said she was sick and hence, unavailable for the police investigation. The police officer forced the girl to come out of her room and as soon as she emerged, it became obvious from her expression that she was guilty. But she would not confess.

Meanwhile, seeing that her legs were smeared with

blood, the police raided her room. A small corner of the room looked as if it had been freshly dug up and then covered, coated, and smeared as it was with fresh cow dung. A corner of the room was full of the leaves and branches of the drumstick tree, known to cause abortions when ingested. Though the police interrogated the girl, she refused to tell the truth.

Then she and her father were arrested and summoned to court. In her statement, the girl finally confessed that a man called Arjun was the child's father and that she had aborted the foetus at home in the fifth month of pregnancy. When Arjun was apprehended, he cunningly shifted blame away from himself. Since the identity of the person who had provided the girl with the medicine of drumstick leaves that caused the abortion could not be proved, the girl was blamed entirely for the abortion, arrested, and jailed at the Dharwad prison. After serving her sentence there, when she was released, she went to Pune and began living with a Parsi man there. Because of her immoral behaviour, her father suffered enormous shame, grief, and guilt right until his old age. Finally, the family left Dharwad.

There are other similar recurrent stories of widows and their immoral conduct in every town within the region. As I send you a description of these cases, I have come to firmly believe that the only solution to

Arjun and the Lady

the problem lies in widow-remarriage. Nothing will ever change for the country unless people change their minds and take it upon themselves to remarry widows. Because powerful landowning castes of southern Maharashtra primarily consist of upper castes, Brahmins, and Marathas, the widows of these regions are horribly oppressed. The Swami Shankaracharya in fact, personally forces widows to undergo tonsure. While women curse and criticize scripture writers who prescribe the tonsuring of widows, their oppression and torture continues. In fact, widows often run away to English cantonment areas and prefer to grow their hair and work as prostitutes there to escape torture. There are at least fifty such cases of widows in this town who have taken recourse to this strategy. I can recount a few names and instances over here.

When the clerk at the Sanglikar landowner's office passed away, his widow was still a twenty-year-old. Her parents and in-laws forcefully tonsured her, but despite that, she started growing her hair back. Seeing this, the landowner punished her by tonsuring her again, and locked her up in a room for three days. But she grew back her hair again and finally, ran away from home. She currently works in this town as a prostitute.

Similarly, the widow of a learned Hindu priest and preacher called Venki from an illustrious family hailing from Misrakot, has started working as a prostitute here. If I start describing all the cases of widows who have turned to prostitution—the life of a *janmasaubhagyavati*, this letter will become too long. So, I will summarize my findings by reiterating that many child-widows from affluent, powerful, and landowning families that boast of social prestige, live extremely tortured personal lives as widows. Whatever will happen, for example, to the delicate, beautiful nine-year-old daughter of Sonikar Vaman-rao Saheb Patwardhan, given in marriage to Ichalkaranjikar Ghorpade Tatya Saheb's son, who died just four days after their marriage? At present, that little girl is only ten years old. How is she going to spend the rest of her life?

Similarly, when one of the Kurunduvadkar brothers died, his wife was just eighteen years old. What will she do now? There is the widow of the Mirajkar family in town. What will be her fate? Whenever the Swami Shankaracharya visits, many of these widows shave their heads in anticipation of his arrival while others just leave town temporarily.

There was a Karhade Brahmin family called Bhat living here. The widow of that family, despite having had four or five children, had an illicit affair and became pregnant. When a scandal broke out, she took medicine to induce an abortion and this medicine proved poisonous for her. She suffered, and died a terrible death. She was hurriedly cremated overnight. A similar incident took place at Pachhapurkar Deshpande's house, as also in Vadikar Inamdar's family.

There are many such women in the region, whose husbands have died within ten years of their marriage. In my village, there are at least a hundred Brahmin widows who have grown back their hair. Emulating useless Brahminical practices, other castes like the Sonar, Prabhu, Vaani, Kasar, Tambat, and Maratha have additionally also begun forcing their daughters and daughters-in-law into the humiliation and the sadness of widowhood. These other Hindu castes cooperate strongly with Brahmins within their regions and try to solder the demographic strength of Brahmins through such practices that also increase their own prestige. The moment a Shudra attains the smallest land title here, he starts calling himself a Maratha landowner, and prohibits the widows in his family from remarrying! A few days ago, when the widow of Kolhapurkar Maharaj had an affair and became pregnant, she was forced to commit suicide after a scandal broke out.

Even though there are a hundred such calamities taking place every day, do these cruel Brahmins who endorse widowhood practices ever spare a thought for the lives of these poor widows? If a widow is caught in an immoral act, she only needs to have enough money to buy off the priest in question.

All these priests charge money to bestow immoral women with salvation. Brahmins meanwhile don't even entertain the idea of widows ever deserving the chance of having a new life with a second husband. They deny and debar widows from wanting to lead a normal, decent life. Instead, she must be obedient like a slave and work like an animal all day, eat only once a day after everyone in the house has had their fill, and that too only a meagre amount. The in-laws are loathe to spend even a rupee on her for a saree or a few other items that she may need. They just wait for her to die.

Those who are poor go and work as servants in other people's houses and even though they are Brahmin, widows are disallowed from entering the house from the front door. They must enter the house from the back door and they must forever be obsequious, flatter and please the *yajman* or the master of the household. They are helpless when outside the house, for even if they cross the road in front of anyone else leaving for work, they are considered an inauspicious omen. They must, therefore, cover their faces and heads entirely when outside the house. I have myself heard so many young child widows say that it would be an enormous boon if Brahmin gurus and spiritual leaders would find a way out in their holy scriptures to save widows from the agony of their suffering.

13

The Moment of Decision

After finishing the letter, Vinayak-*rao* said to his audience: 'So, my good sirs! What is the reason for all these problems in the Brahmin community? Apart from the irrationality of Brahminism, what are the reasons for disallowing widow-remarriage? If widows are not tortured and do not suffer as you say, then what is the reason for this anarchy? If on the other hand, they were allowed to respectfully remarry, would they ever engage in such activities? You say that the British government is oppressive. On the other hand, should you not be grateful to the British government for rescuing our widowed daughters and daughters-in-law from such horrible accidents, turmoil, and misdeeds? Now, Keshav-*rao-ji*, what is your opinion about the contents of this letter?'

Keshav-*rao*: 'I am unable to say it is false, since such incidents also take place in Satara. But I don't think we should go to the other extreme of allowing widow-remarriage. There is no scriptural permission for it, and we can hardly oppose our religion, can we! Maybe we should ask the others present here. What do our scriptures say about widow-remarriage, Krushna-*shastri*?'

Quoting a Sanskrit verse from the *Manusmriti*, Krushna-*shastri* said: 'Manu says that once the marriage ritual of *kanyadaan* is fulfilled, this ritual should not be performed for the same girl again.'

Another guest, Vireshwar-*shastri* interjected: 'You are misinterpreting this injunction since its true meaning, in fact, supports widow-remarriage. The verse actually means that a father is disallowed from breaking his promise of *kanyadaan* made to one groom, by marrying his daughter and giving her in *kanyadaan* to another groom. On doing this, he can be accused of breaking a promise and of perpetuating falsehoods. The meaning of this verse cannot be extended to an injunction disallowing widows from remarrying after their first husbands have died. In fact, there are other scriptural references that can be interpreted as being supportive of widow-remarriage. If we were to accept those, we can allow widow-remarriage and provide relief to many suffering widows.'

Keshav-*rao*: 'Even if such instances favouring widow-remarriage occur within religious scriptures, there is no ritual description of widow-remarriage. Since there are no prescribed marriage rituals described for widows, it is difficult to allow it.'

Vinayak-*rao*: 'Your argument defies common sense. If ritual descriptions of widow-remarriage are absent from Hindu scriptures, does that allow you to conclude that widow-remarriage is against the Hindu religion? Then, does the same Hindu religion specifically allow for widows to suffer alone without husbands, allow for the murder of infants, and for their immorality?'

Vishveshwar-*shastri*: 'It is not compulsory to chant *mantra*s or perform rituals at each and every marriage ceremony. The ritual act of *panigrahan* itself connotes marriage since it prescribes the placing of the bride and bridegroom's hands together.'

Jagannath-*ji* retorted: 'Oh yes, so we should now follow the marriage practices of Englishmen, is it? I once attended an English wedding in a church in Mumbai out of curiosity. The husband and wife held hands and the priest said, "Now, I have married you to each other. It is a union that God has blessed, and no man can break it." The bride and groom placed rings on each other's fingers. Shastri-*baba* here, having studied in an English school in Pune, is now advising us to institute English practices in our own marriage rituals.'

Vishveshwar-*shastri* replied: 'But what if this practice is contained within our own Hindu scriptures?'

Jagannath-*ji* asked Moro-*shastri*: 'What do you think, Shastri? Are there such injunctions in our Hindu scriptures?'

Moro-*shastri* replied: 'Not that I can remember!'

Then Vireshwar-*shastri* said: 'According to the Smriti texts, one cannot accept another as a husband by just pronouncing it to be true. The ritual of *panigrahan* or hands being placed within hands is what decides the identity of husband and wife. Now, is this practice English? Or is this practice Hindu? No one knows! But since such injunctions exist in Hindu texts, what is wrong in following it to get widows remarried?'

Keshav-*rao*: 'Even if what you say is correct, how can we ever imagine breaking an ancient tradition? This is improper!'

Vinayak-*rao*: 'But you have broken other ancient traditions by now to help you live your everyday life! Can't you think of other prominent Hindu traditions that are broken nowadays, that you so easily tolerate?'

Vireshwar-*shastri*: 'There are many such scriptural practices. For example, and I will enumerate a few by quoting the relevant Sanskrit scriptures, there is an injunction that outcasts those Hindus who sit in a boat and cross the ocean. But this practice is nowadays easily broken as thousands of Hindus sit in boats and travel to Dwarka, Kutch, and other Konkani port towns. Didn't our famous Hindu lawyer Rango-*pant*

The Moment of Decision

just return from England? Wasn't he accepted back into his caste? Secondly, there is a strict injunction against long periods of *brahmacharya* or scholarly asceticism in Kaliyuga. But don't so many Brahmins practice lifelong scholarly asceticism and remain celibate? In fact, they are considered honourable and are respected for doing so. Lastly, even if threatened with poverty, Brahmins in Kaliyuga are strictly forbidden from engaging in any professional activity that is the prerogative of another caste like the Kshatriya or Vaishya. They are disallowed from wielding any weapons or engaging in trading or business. Yet, we know many Brahmins, who engage in such professions for their livelihoods. No one stops them. If we are to disallow widow-remarriage because of ambiguity within the Hindu scriptures, we should certainly disallow every Brahmin from travelling, practising celibacy, or engaging in Kshatriya and Vaishya professions. But Brahmin men think nothing of it all nowadays and don't harbour any fear or guilt about breaking these religious rules. Neither does anyone blame them. So, why are widows being singled out? Why has widow-remarriage become the domain where all the dignity of Hindus is being held at stake, or their scriptures perceived as threatened? Why should we insist on irrational behaviour?'

Vinayak-*rao*: 'If our conference is unable to arrive at a decision despite the arguments presented, it would have proved a waste of time to discuss all this today. All the knowledgeable Hindu reformers and scholars of this town are gathered here tonight. I would hence request you to consider the suffering of widows in our county and alleviate it. We must decide tonight.'

Jagannath: 'But it is so late. I would suggest you to leave this debate here. We can decide next time we meet.'

Vireshwar-*shastri*: 'It is rather late—almost past one in the night. But if this had been a musical soiree, it would not have been considered so late! Even the early hours of the morning would have been considered too early. In any case, I am happy that it is the righteous argument that has won the debate tonight.'

Vinayak-*rao*: 'Yes, when we strike a flint, sparks are bound to fly! But despite this, we must be grateful and happy that the truth prevails.'

Jagannath: 'You can hardly decide that on your own! We all have to participate in that decision, don't we? Your victory depends on what we all decide. Not on who won the argument tonight. But it is true that we have had a strong argument. What an occasion for it! I wouldn't have dreamed that an evening of entertainment and celebration would end up becoming an evening of intellectual arguments and hot reformist debate.'

Saying this, Jagannath concluded the evening's celebration by asking his nephew to distribute betel-leaf and betel-nut to all those present. All the guests congratulated Jagannath once again and left.

What must, however, be noted, was the absolute politeness and courtesy with which the debate and argument about widow-remarriage had proceeded. One of the reasons for this was that the Brahmins who had come for alms and charity that evening had gradually left after the evening's entertainment show was cancelled. So, the crowd was thin in any case, allowing the discussion to take place among the well-educated, renowned, and knowledgeable scholars, priests, government servants, and student scholars of that town.

14

Death

It was already the next day when Yamuna-*bai* finally found the opportunity of asking Vinayak-*rao* about what had transpired in the discussion the earlier evening. The discussion had proceeded till so late that she had fallen asleep by the time he had returned. However, after hearing everything, she realized that the conference had proved useless.

She said: 'Your conference seems more like the council of mice from *Aesop's Fables*! Though the suggestion of tying a bell round the cat's neck was smart, the idea failed because none came forward to tie that bell. Similarly, you all arrived at a consensus of allowing widow-remarriage, but since no one wanted to implement it, such consensus could be theoretically achieved a million times over, but without effect. If those in power; those who control money, and receive an education don't take any initiative to act on their ideas, then how would the misery of widows ever be alleviated? Who should help the poor? The poor themselves? How do those who utilize government funds for education and training justify themselves? What do they return to society? After all, the government expects very little from them. The only aim of imparting them education, if at all, is for them to develop their own society—especially in those religious domains where the government cannot interfere. Instead, these people are busy negotiating large monetary transactions for personal benefit that further consolidate their own selfish gains. Some are degraded enough to pretend to be reformers and build a grand, impressive aura; but only till their work gets done. Once they get what they want, they finally abandon the masquerade with alacrity, either avoiding such discussions in future or even contradicting and criticizing reform. Your friend Jagannath seems to be of that ilk.'

Vinayak-*rao* had no option but to quietly hear out Yamuna-*bai*'s angry words. He had no argument to defend his friend. She was right.

He said: 'Since Jagannath-*ji* is from the Sonar caste, he is afraid that if he supports reform, he will lose face within his community. Nowadays, Sonars want to become Brahmins by imitating Brahmin rituals. They think behaving like Brahmins or imitating them, will bestow them upper-caste or quasi-Brahmin status. Given this problem of wanting to be upwardly mobile in terms of caste, how on earth can we expect Sonars to ever support widow-remarriage? They pander instead, to Brahmins. In Mumbai at least, it is no longer possible to distinguish Sonars from Brahmins. Sonar rituals and practices of widowhood are exactly like Brahmin rituals and Sonars get offended if referred to by the epithet '*Shet*' or merchant. Now, they want everyone to use the epithet '*Bhat*' or Brahmin. With all this foolishness of caste arrogance, it would perhaps be beneath their dignity to accept Maratha caste practices of widow-remarriage. What ridiculous notions! They are ruining their own lives and alongside that, the lives of others. In any case, let it be now. We have wasted too much time over here as it is, and need to hurry home. Our family must be awaiting us. I want to leave tomorrow itself.'

Yamuna-*bai*, understanding her husband's wishes, began packing for their onward journey and the couple, after bidding Jagannath farewell, set off for home. As they reached Jejuri, their servants rushed ahead, searching for a halting place for the night. The cart driver stopped the cart by the wayside and went to a nearby well for water. Shivram, the little boy from Pandharpur, who had joined them with his mother, sat languidly in the cart driver's seat, fiddling

Death

with the reins. It was a hot afternoon and Vinayak-*rao* had loaned the boy his umbrella. Now, because the boy opened the large umbrella with a jerk, the bulls suddenly grew startled. They reared in panic and then, dashed the cart off into a nearby ditch.

While the boy and Yamuna-*bai* fell off the cart due to the tremendous jolt, one of the cart's wheels ran over Shivram's thigh. Yamuna-*bai* was mostly unhurt as she fell onto a pile of ashes. The jolt was, however, strong enough for the inside wedge of the cart to ram itself hard into Vinayak-*rao*'s ribcage. Hearing the commotion, the servants and cart driver came running and with much effort, lifted the cart out of the ditch.

Steering it back onto the road and with the help of some villagers, they brought Vinayak-*rao* to the place where they were supposed to halt overnight. They were delayed in Jejuri as the cart had to be first repaired with the help of the village carpenter. Though Shivram recovered quickly after his swollen thigh was bandaged with turmeric, Yamuna could hardly think about herself in this time as Vinayak-*rao* was seriously wounded. Hearing her dearest husband moan and cry out in pain, Yamuna's heart wrenched in the deepest of turmoil. While Vinayak-*rao*'s side did not hurt as much the first day, the pain and swelling intensified over the next few days. There was no medicine available in the village and neither did Jejuri have its own doctor or *vaidya*. So, Vinayak-*rao* was rushed to Nasik in a palanquin. Though his medical treatment in Nasik commenced immediately, the intense pain in his side refused to subside. His parents became terrified and started weeping and beating their chests in the grief and fear of losing their only son!

But who would describe Yamuna-*bai*'s private grief? She loved her husband dearly and the couple never disagreed on anything and never felt disappointed with each other. They were both secure and confident persons and agreed on all issues. They were perfectly matched—a rarity. Their biggest shared trait was their concern for the wellbeing of the soul. Yamuna-*bai* at least, had spent her whole childhood studying, and contemplating the importance of the soul. With her grace and in her sweet, persuasive way, she had gradually turned Vinayak-*rao*'s heart towards religion too. They had both begun believing in the same religion and in the truth of the redeemer. It had been their wish, at least Yamuna-*bai*'s wish, to convert to this religion that she had secretly followed in her heart for so long.

When this very spiritually-inclined couple suffered such sudden calamity, they decided to bear this grief as stoically as possible. Yamuna-*bai* did not leave her husband's side even once and whenever the *vaidya* visited to renew Vinayak-*rao*'s medications, she would describe the latter's condition in detail so as to save her husband the effort of speaking. She took all possible care, minutely overseeing his food and medication, and she kept his clothes and bed scrupulously clean. She sat next to him all day, making cheerful conversion that entertained and encouraged him.

One afternoon, the *vaidya* lowered his head in frustration and fell into deep thought as he beheld Vinaya-*rao*'s deteriorating health. When he started discussing a new plan of medical treatment, Yamuna-*bai* asked him point blank: '*Dada*, what do you think about his health?'

The *vaidya* said: '*Bai*, I have left no stone unturned in treating him.'

Yamuna-*bai* turned to her husband and said in a sad voice: 'My dearest, I feel you are about to abandon me after all! What will be my condition after you go away? You sheltered me from the world. Now, whom shall I turn to? How will I continue without you? I hope God heals you quickly.'

Hearing this, Vinayak-*rao* spoke in a weak voice: 'My darling! If God so wishes that I leave you, then I must accept His wish. But perhaps you will be happy to hear that I have been contemplating and worrying about the state of my soul in the past few days. Even though in the past you repeatedly asked me to consider this in your usual loving way, I did not pay much heed. Like many of my other friends, I was careless. Though I tried to imbibe good values and lead a moral life, I was not a *bhakta* of God. I was busy with material acquisitions. I was concerned about reform, but not about *bhakti*. While the welfare of human beings troubled me, I did nothing to spread God's word. Now I repent this bitterly! If only God were to have mercy on me and give me a few more years to live, I will spend my remaining life in His service. I will dedicate myself to Him, body and soul. But I slowly lose hope now. I don't know what to do.'

Yamuna-*bai* was spellbound as she sat listening to Vinayak-*rao*'s words. Finally, she said: 'We are both guilty of tremendous sin, and we both deserve God's punishment. We spent the best years of our lives in the pursuit of material pleasures. It was only when sorrows and worries besieged, impaired, and laid us low, that we thought of God. We are abominable sinners! Still, God is kind and merciful, slow to anger, and eager to shower us with His blessings. He won't argue endlessly, and neither will He nurture rage against us. He has gifted us pure thoughts even in a difficult time like this, and the presence of these thoughts are already a sign of his mercy. We don't deserve this kindness! My darling, even if you leave me now and go ahead of me, I am sure we will be reunited in heaven. Promise me that you will meet me again in heaven.'

Vinayak-*rao*: 'How can I redeem myself? How will my sins ever be forgiven?'

Yamuna-*bai*: 'Please don't be agitated. You learned so many things as part of your education. Try to remember the verses of the Scriptures that comfort and encourage you. Try also to gratefully remember our Lord Jesus Christ, who died on the cross for us. He calls out to us now, full of mercy, and says, "I will never abandon those who approach me. Everyone is invited to come to me and I will redeem them all. That person who has faith in me, he will live even after passing away and gain eternal life." Our redeemer is so close to us and we experience His presence through His words. Since He has proved Himself to be true, having faith in Him is a really easy task. Trust God, and He will forgive us all our sins!'

Vinayak-*rao*: 'It is through these words that I perceive God's brilliance and strength. Every other way is useless.'

Yamuna-*bai*: 'The pure Holy Spirit reveals God's powers of redemption, His glory and beauty to us. His rays of light penetrate our soul and remove all the darkness of suspicion lurking therein.'

In this way, Yamuna-*bai* soothed her husband with

the hope of God's mercy. In the meanwhile, the cook brought in his diet and seeing that he was dozing after having eaten a little, Yamuna left Vinayak-*rao*'s bedside and climbed up to the loft, where she could sit and pray alone.

There, she sat in solitude and prayed with her whole heart to her heavenly father thus: 'Oh, my purest, dearest father, your roads are straightforward and just. You have a plan for us and you desire our happiness. Dear God, you are never wrong, and you never bring us misery. You don't wish death even on sinners! Dear God, it is due to your blessings that I recognize your love. I praise you. I am overjoyed to be blessed by your only son, Lord Jesus Christ. Dear merciful God, please heal my husband from this terrible illness. I would be orphaned if he were to die. Look to me with compassion and look to him with mercy. If it be your wish that he should live for some more years to serve you, then please heal him. And if this is not what you wish, then, dear God, please have mercy on his soul. I will be eternally grateful to you for opening his eyes and awakening his soul. Dear Father, please allow him to understand the meaning of the sacrifice your only son Lord Jesus Christ made for the redemption of humankind. And let him have strong belief in our Lord. Even if we are separated now, we will meet in heaven and never be separated

Death

again. Oh, my dearest Lord Jesus Christ, please accept my prayer. *Hey Bhagawan*! Please hold my hand as I walk through deep waters. Please protect me as I walk over burning coals. Dear God, whom should I approach in this time of need but you? You support all those in suffering and in pain and help them. Oh God, please heed my request. I beg you to answer.'

As she prayed, Yamuna-*bai*'s eyes filled with tears and she was overcome with emotion. For a while she sat there in silence. And in this silence, she heard a small, soft note—a few whispered words that were full of encouragement, as if someone was standing right next to her and speaking.

She clearly heard the words: 'Don't fear, for I am with you! Don't be afraid, for I am your God and will give you strength. I will help you.'

Hearing these words, Yamuna felt her strength and courage return. She climbed down from the loft, ate a little and then, returned to Vinayak-*rao*'s bedside. Seeing him sleeping, she picked up a book and sat there next to him, reading quietly to herself.

Waking up, he asked: 'My dear, what are you reading?'

She answered: 'I am reading Psalm 71 from the Book of Psalms. Should I read out to you?'

Vinayak-*rao*: 'Yes, please! I would love to listen to some of the couplets—a few *ovya*.'

Yamuna-*bai* began reading: 'Dear God, I have placed my hope in you, and in doing so, may I never regret! May your mercy remove my difficulties and protect me. Hear my words and redeem me. May I spend my life with those by whom you stand. You have promised to redeem me. You are my rock and you are my fortress. Oh dear God, protect me from those wicked and from the cruel hands of the oppressor. You are my only hope...'

As she continued reading, Vinayak-*rao* interrupted her. He was equally overcome and said that the many couplets she read filled his heart with a special peace and courage: 'God is indeed my rock, and He is indeed my fortress. If I stay with Him, no one can frighten me! I would no longer feel scared.'

Yamuna-*bai*: 'This is how we develop faith in God's redemption. Our experiences change us and we begin to feel God's forgiveness of our sins. This strengthens our faith as we begin seeing His straightforward path.'

Vinayak-*rao*: 'I am grateful and thankful to God for having given you this wisdom. I feel regretful and ashamed for having avoided faith so far; I repent it now. I should have been the one to learn it and even teach it to you; but instead, I focused more on worldly knowledge and avoided spiritual wisdom. What a fool I have been! May God have mercy upon me; may He forgive me my sins; and may He care for my soul at death. My dearest wife, I don't think I will live for too long now. I don't feel afraid of death, but I feel afraid for you. Considering the mentality of the people here fills me with the worry of you being alone with them. They will torture you and never respect your wishes. Knowing all the terrible difficulties of a widow's life, I am horrified that these problems will now come to confront my poor dear, young and talented wife. These people will never allow you to remarry. They would rather let you suffer a million humiliations and sorrows for the rest of your life. They would find it sweet to pit you into darkness and crush you under the burden of menial tasks and servitude, but never give you the freedom to resettle your life. They would hate to see you happy, to see your knowledge and wisdom grow and to see that you have another husband to love and care of you. They would prefer to disfigure you and turn you into a scapegoat that everyone will revile. Only that will make them feel they have completed their religious duties.'

Yamuna-*bai*: 'Please don't worry, dear husband. I have known for a while that I cannot find happiness here. And it is not that I want to save myself from physical suffering. It is because they will never allow me to follow my path of *bhakti* and serve God, that I can't find happiness here. But don't worry. Even if I were a widow, the Lord who cares for all orphans and widows will also protect me. I have placed my entire trust in Him, and I am certain He won't abandon me. The only thing that causes me pain and sorrow is to see you go and be separated from you so early in life. The night is nearly over and when the dawn comes, we will stand in front of our redeemer, our hearts filled with joy, our smiles radiant!'

Saying this, she read out passages from the fourteenth chapter of John, and from the twenty-sixth and twenty-seventh chapters of Mathew and wondered aloud about God's enormous love for human beings. Soon however, Vinayak-*rao*'s face turned pale. He understood that God's messenger had come to take him. A painful arrow of love suddenly pierced his heart, and he was briefly in turmoil calling out to the Lord Jesus Christ to save him from the pain. After that, he peacefully left the world that was but momentary and transitioned into the next world that was full of eternal joy.

15

The Gathering of Clouds

Vinayak-*rao*'s family was amazed at Yamuna-*bai*'s Christian fortitude, despite her terrible grief. She had desisted from weeping loudly like other widows. Neither had she blamed or abused God for her fate. Though utterly grief-stricken, she had held God's peace in her heart, which gave her hope and strength.

She would sit in solitude for hours and meditate thus: 'God is my father and my husband. Even though he has taken away my support and hope in this earthly life, I know he draws closer. I know I will not live here for too long now. These days of sorrows shall pass and soon, I will be happy again. I love God ever more, for by taking away my darling husband, He allows me to give Him my heart. From now on, I dedicate my heart and soul to God.'

Even as she sat alone thinking all this, her family conspired against her. They noticed the change in her—after all, was it not natural for the light of faith that had ignited her heart to cascade over into the world around her? But darkness hates the touch of light, for light and darkness are natural enemies. Yamuna's in-laws had taken note of her different nature from the very beginning and had disliked her independence. Now that her only support had departed, Yamuna's mother-in-law was sanguine that she was trapped and could be treated whichever way she liked. In his last days, Vinayak-*rao* had requested his father to promise that they wouldn't tonsure Yamuna. And therefore, no one initially said anything about Yamuna's hair when he was cremated.

But as time passed, Yamuna's mother-in-law began torturing Yamuna. She would ensure that the girl was forced to do the roughest and heaviest of housework and though Yamuna never complained, her mother-in-law began abusing her at the slightest of pretexts. Following her example, the other women of the household also began reviling Yamuna. Eating the food she cooked was out of the question, as no one even drank water from her hands anymore. Yamuna tolerated it all, but with growing surprise. Were these the same people who had once showered her with adoration?

The next event was the arrival of the family priest Moro-*bhatta* to the house. He had gone to another village for some months and was now back to visit Vinayak-*rao*'s father, who was an old client, his *yajman*. After visiting Vinayak-*rao*'s father in the front room of the house, he went inside to sit with Yamuna's mother-in-law. Seeing him, Vinayak-*rao*'s mother began weeping for her son, recounting all his good qualities.

Moro-*bhatta*: 'Yes, your son was a fine man. He was humble despite all his talents and good qualities. Whatever can we do now! His death is a great tragedy. No one could have imagined that he would be so short-lived. This is fate! No one can avert God's will. It is useless to mourn him now. Yamuna has to bear the fate of living as a widow now. Is she here? Or has she returned to her father's house?'

Yamuna's mother-in-law: 'She is here alright, sitting inside her room. She has no one left in her father's house now. Her father, immersed in debt, had to work as repayment of his debts in Baroda and he hasn't returned as yet.'

Moro-*bhatta*: 'Then, how do we proceed with her widowhood rituals? I had already advised you to complete her rituals at the time of her husband's cremation. Is that decision still lagging?'

Lady: 'What can I say? As a woman I hardly have a say over my husband's will! I too had suggested that we best do the rituals at the time of his cremation, and cremate Yamuna's husband's rightful belongings—her hair with him. But my son extracted a deathbed promise from his father of not tonsuring her, and so my husband remained true to his word. But now there is no such problem. Since some time has passed now, what is the difficulty in tonsuring her? Or is there any? I am afraid that if we continue to hold on to meaningless promises, we may face ruination.'

Moro-*bhatta*: 'I hope you made no such promises to your son on your part!'

Lady: 'Not at all! What an idea! Why should I place a noose around my own neck? I was waiting for you all these days. Good that you have come at last…'

Moro-*bhatta*: 'These days are difficult. It is tough to estimate what new laws about widowhood the government will suddenly implement. In the last two months in Pune, I heard that the government was about to pass a widow-remarriage law.'

Lady: 'Oh, my God! What new depravity is this? Those dratted Englishmen will ask us to convert our daughters and marry them to Christians next!'

Moro-*bhatta*: 'That day is not too far! I only pray that we don't have to see this disaster taking place in front of our own eyes.'

Lady: 'Yes, we will resist it tooth and nail. But once we die, who cares?'

Moro-*bhatta*: 'So, tell me, what about her widowhood rituals now?'

Lady: 'About Yamuna? I will follow whatever instructions you issue.'

Moro-*bhatta*: 'I think we should tonsure her as soon as possible. Then she won't ever dare to raise her eyes and look at another man.'

Lady: 'Is there any special ritual involved?'

Moro-*bhatta*: 'Nothing specific. We are still at the same place of her husband's death. So, there is no need to go anywhere else for the ritual. We will take her to the river, worship her in a small ceremony there, smear her forehead with vermillion, and ritually fill her lap with gifts for the last time. Placing *durva* on her head, the barber will remove her hair according to the presiding Brahmin's instructions. Half the price of the jewellery and clothes she wears on that day will be paid as fees to the barber and then a small effigy of her husband made from dough will be burned at the cremation ground along with her hair and bangles. She should finish her own death rituals with her hands, and after a mourning period of three days, commence living her life as a widow.'

Lady: 'Yes, exactly! But what about that promise?'

Moro-*bhatta*: 'I will console your husband. Don't worry! But we must finish the ritual as soon as possible, so that her forward path of remarriage can be blocked.

There is the danger of that new law coming into action soon; it will bring a storm upon us.'

Lady: 'You should prescribe some daily rules for her. She will remain busy with that and her mind will not be diverted. In the meanwhile, we will arrange for her tonsuring rituals.'

Moro-*bhatta*: 'I will bring the *Gurucharitra* along with me tomorrow. There is a long passage in it about the correct behaviour prescribed for widows. I will read the instructions aloud to your husband and to Yamuna. That should put pay on all their objections. This religious text is of tremendous importance and value! Who would disrespect it?'

Lady: 'Well, if you can convey all this to them, then the achievement and its credit are entirely yours. You will have relieved me of all my worries. I can't even begin to describe that girl's posturing nowadays, her arrogance. Though she works silently, she rushes off to my son's room whenever she finds the time, sits on his cot and reads his books. My husband has stopped concerning himself with her behaviour from the very day of our son's death. After all, she was his dear friend's daughter! So, he ignores her ways and says nothing. It is I, who has to tolerate it all.'

Moro-*bhatta*: 'It is true. The whole burden falls on you! Well, I must leave now, for it gets late and I still have to visit another client for their *Ekadashi* ritual. That reminds me—the day after tomorrow is an ideal occasion for reading the *Gurucharitra*, since it is *pradosh*—an auspicious occasion for religious tasks that demand stoicism and solemnity.'

Saying this, Moro-*bhatji* left. Though Yamuna-*bai* had heard him and her mother-in-law speaking in lowered tones and sotto voice, she had not understood their words. But whatever little she understood was enough to tell her that a calamity was just about to befall her, a serpent waiting to strike. The time had come, for testing her faith in religion and in God.

Just as she sat contemplating this, the boy Shivram ran up to her and gave her a letter. Opening it, but not recognizing the signature, Yamuna read on:

Dear Sister,

Please don't consider me a stranger even though you don't recognize my name. I am an old friend of your husband's and we were greatly fond of each other. It was from him that I first heard of you. I am extremely sorry to hear about his death and can only imagine the tragedy you face now. I would be betraying my friend if I did not write to you in such a time of sorrow. Therefore, forgive me for writing to you so directly as we have not been formally introduced as yet.

May God give me the right words to express my condolences and I wish for His peace and wisdom to prevail upon you in these difficult times. May the Holy Spirit reside within you as you read these words. In ancient times, God told His servants, 'even as sorrows are many, so are the consolations of the Lord Jesus Christ.' May you be blessed! My heart fills with pain every time I think of your sorrow, especially as I know that you are of delicate health and of a sensitive predisposition. If not for God who has blessed you with special strength and courage, you would by now have already drowned in a sea of turmoil and hopelessness. But I have experienced God to be all-powerful and trustworthy and you must also have this experience. Therefore, I say unto you, as Daniel said to the king, 'that God whom you pray to; He will come and loosen your bonds.' God is eternally merciful, and though He has taken away your dearest person, it is only to give you double that grace in the future. Even as a stream dries up, it is rewarded by a waterfall—God's own presence. He is that eternal waterfall.

God gave you the happiness of a wonderful husband; and it is He who also has the power to bestow you with the greatest of peace and joy. Your husband has preceded you in death but he has gone to God. And you must remain hopeful about following him to God one day. All unhappiness will then be gone forever. God will wipe away your tears and strengthen your *bhakti* to remain innocent, pure, eternal, and unfragmented. It is only then that you will understand that the unhappiness you suffered was for your own good. These trials are given to you by God and planned by Him in all His wisdom, mercy, and compassion.

God knows your weakness and vulnerability. He will not burden you with a pain greater than you can bear. Instead, He will give you the strength to bear the pain you now feel. No burden or punishment is ever pleasurable. It causes sorrow. But it also teaches and finally imparts the sufferer with peace. So now, steady your lifeless hands and strengthen your shaking knees; use God's strength to gather your own courage. Get up and start walking in his path. I will stop here now as you are immersed in pain. I will pray for you and ask God to free your way ahead and give you the wisdom to take the right decision. I will quote the same words that God's angel used to advise Lot and may those words keep reverberating in your mind: 'Run for your life and don't ever look back! Don't hide in a corner or underneath a cover! Run to the mountains or else, you will be ruined!' Dear lady, I would have written much earlier but I was away in another town; I have just come to learn of your loss.

Yamuna was overjoyed; her happiness at these words knew no bounds. God had helped her by sending her a powerful message of hope and His presence had provided her with courage and confidence. She thanked Him immediately and began hoping for the moment of release and redemption. She hoped to join a community of believers and declare her secretly-held religion to the whole world. She would loudly proclaim God, the Lord Jesus Christ, and sing His praises openly. As such thoughts raced through her mind, she was transported and overcome with joy, and even if for a moment, forgot all her sorrows. Her eyes overflowing with tears, she sang a beautiful, melodious hymn in her low, soft, and pleasant voice:

> I will sing of my merciful God's love.
> I will sing His prayers through happiness and sorrow.
> My heart fills with joy as I come to His refuge.
> Unite in His refuge, oh meek! For over is your despair!
> Go to Him with gratitude that overflows your heart.
> For it was He who redeemed you when you called.
> His divine messengers protect all devotees, all *bhakta*s.
> Trust in Him, oh children of God.

After singing, she read Psalm 23: 'God is my shepherd, and I shall not lack in anything. He places me in tender sunlight and takes me across the calm waters. In His name, He leads me to tread on righteous paths. Even when I walk the narrow valley shadowed by death, I forget all my fear, for He walks with me. His staff is my strength. He oils my hair and lays out a feast for me in the face of my enemies. My cup is full and my days are filled with his joy, glory, and mercy. I will live forever in God's house!'

Every word that Yamuna read felt as priceless as rubies and she trusted God evermore. In that moment, she believed completely that God was by her side and that the Lord Jesus Christ was holding her hand and leading her on His path. He was saying, as in the verse of Revelations 3.8-10: 'Get up now, my child! You still have some strength left in you. You have followed my teachings and I shall protect you henceforth from the trials that await you.'

16

The Final Twist

Yamuna now awaited the battle that drew ever closer, trying to draw succour from her faith and trust in God's mercy. The next day, his ablutions completed, and dressed in his finest ritual attire, Moro-*bhatta* arrived punctually carrying the religious text along with him, the *Gurucharitra*, wrapped carefully in a silk scarf. Yamuna's mother-in-law had prepared for his arrival by clearing the central courtyard, smearing it with cow dung and decorating it with *rangoli*. She had set a seat for Moro-*bhatta* in the middle of the courtyard. Moro-*bhatta* took his seat accompanied by Yamuna's father-in-law there, and after praising the ancient nature and high moral worth of the *Gurucharitra*, began reading from it. Yamuna was instructed by her mother-in-law to sit and listen to the reading from inside the threshold of her room. The summarized chapter written in old Marathi commenced in the following manner:

The Final Twist

The Guru prescribes a way for widows. If the husband and wife be together when the husband dies, it is law that they should proceed together to the pyre. But if pregnant, or the wife still an infant, then she should not be cremated. It is a great sin to breastfeed after widowhood. If the husband dies far away, cremating her is forbidden. She should live as a meritorious widow, as widowhood is of the same virtue as being cremated. After widowhood, she should get the hair from her head removed. For if she retains it, her hair binds her husband's soul and takes him to hell. She must bathe at dawn, eat once a day, and devoutly fast. She must eat only one sort of grain at one time and she should fast for five days especially in the ancestral month of Pitrupaksha by eating only one morsel after moonrise. She should eat by following the moon cycle: two morsels on the first day, increasing the morsel count for the next fifteen days of the bright half.

She can eat a full meal on the full moon day. The morsel count should decrease in the next fifteen days of the dark half till she eats only one morsel on new moon. She must not gain strength and must eat only enough to exist and breathe. She should eat fruit, raw vegetables, or take milk. She should not tolerate impure food. If she sleeps on a cot, her husband suffers in hell. She cannot celebrate festivals, wear fine clothes, bangles, or ornaments. She cannot anoint her face and she must avoid flowers. If she does not have a son, she should perform penance. She must worship the deity Vishnu, perform his rituals, and consider only him to be her husband henceforth. She should go on pilgrimage, fast, donate money and material, and worship gurus. She should donate all she once enjoyed as a married woman to Brahmins. She should constantly worship Shiva and other pure persons. She should feed and donate to them in the name of her husband. She should worship the footwear of ascetics and never wear footwear herself. She should not eat in brass pots and avoid auspicious items, and donate them instead. She should sleep on the ground and donate a cot to pure persons.

Whatever she renounces, she should give away to Brahmins. She should renounce sweets and donate cows. She should feed sweets to Brahmins. She should not wear warm clothing during winter and donate these to Brahmins instead. She should not use blankets but give these to Brahmins. She should not take medicine when she falls ill in winters, but donate foods that generate heat to Brahmins. She should never sit in a cart. She should wear only white clothes. If she has a son, she should be under his command. This is the ideal behaviour of a widow. Her bhakti for her husband must remain unfailing. Even if he is a sinner and dies early to live in hell like an insect, her behaviour as a widow redeems him of his sins. At her death, she takes him along with her to heaven.

Though Moro-*bhatta* was no *puranik*, he postured and pretended to be one. But it was also a time of

The Final Twist

sorrow for Vinayak-*rao*'s family. His parents' wounds were still fresh and they could not appreciate the reading. Ganesh-*pant* was continually overwhelmed, his eyes filling with tears many times. Though Vinayak-*rao*'s mother felt bad too, her dislike for Yamuna and her insistence that she should be tonsured forthwith prevailed over her grief as she allowed Moro-*bhatta* to complete. After Moro-*bhatta* finished reading and worshipping his text, he accepted his payment for it in cash and grain.

He said to Ganesh-*pant*: 'We should finish Yamuna's widowhood rituals as soon as possible. These are mandated and meritorious rituals that must be completed to prevent the dead person's torture in the after-world. And being responsible for this torture is a great stigma for the dead person's family in this world.'

Moro-*bhatta* tried to convince his *yajman* to carry out Yamuna's tonsuring ritual on the next month anniversary of Vinayak-*rao*'s death. He suggested that Yamuna be taken to the river and her hair be removed and cremated there. After that, she would have to compulsorily follow the injunctions for widows mandated by the *Gurucharitra* that Moro-*bhatta* had just read out. But Ganesh-*pant* had deep affection for Yamuna, and he choked on his tears at the very thought of tonsuring her as the reading came to an end.

He exclaimed: 'Yamuna, my dear girl! You must now accept whatever is in your fate. Even if you have never wronged anyone, you have just heard what a great sin it is for you to keep your hair. My dear girl, you are still youthful, charming, and beautiful. Your husband was so very fond of you. And this is what we are reduced to today, just a couple of months after his back is turned! I never thought I would ever live see you so degraded and that too in my own house. Oh, my God! What have we come to! Oh, my dear son Vinayak! Where did you go away leaving us here in this condition? I dread what I have to witness now in your absence. Oh, what a horrible state!'

As Ganesh-*pant* continued to lament, Moro-*bhatta* said: '*Rao-ji*, this is hardly the time to grieve! Whose daughter? And whose son? These are all finally crows sitting on the roof. Where are your children from your past birth? Do you know them? They take birth on their own and die alone on their own. Your children are born because they are tied to you through a debt from their past life. Having repaid this, they are freed and they depart. What is the use of grieving now? It is useless to harbour any worldly attachment! Come, we will go out into the veranda and sit there. Your agitation will only grow if the girl lingers in front of your eyes.'

The Final Twist

Saying this, Moro-*bhatta* took Ganesh-*pant* outside and was himself preparing to leave, when Ganesh-*pant* declared: 'I am against tonsuring Yamuna. I had promised this to my son Vinayak and I cannot break this promise now! Moreover, the girl is humble and good natured. I don't want to brand her and disfigure her with any further sorrow. The scriptures you have read out, they are ancient and do not fit into our current times. And I don't mind if I don't follow them at all.'

Ganesh-*pant*'s wife, who was standing just inside the door, angrily retorted: 'So, what are we supposed to do now? Do you want to get the girl remarried or what? Then do just that! It will certainly improve your reputation in society! Watch the fun unfold! Our golden boy has gone and we suffer from the burden of that sorrow. Now, let us invite new sorrows upon us, so that we can be crushed under the weight of its worry. If we keep her un-tonsured in this way, it is I who will face embarrassment in society. It is I who will be cornered from all sides.'

Moro-*bhatta*: 'Lady, please don't be agitated. *Yajman* is a man of a different and sensitive mindset. But he is also sensible. He will not insult the advice of the knowledgeable by disregarding their words. I will bring Deshmukh here with me tomorrow. He has just arrived from Wai. He enjoys tremendous status as a

Brahmin and is celebrated for the vast expanse of his knowledge. I am sure *yajman* would want a second opinion made by another knowledgeable person. It will help him to make up his mind and arrive at a firm decision.'

Ganesh-*pant*: 'I would be greatly relieved to meet Deshmukh. I had become introduced to him through my son. I will definitely not disregard his opinion. I have no objection to logical arguments.'

In this way Moro-*bhatji* left, keying up the household and creating as much tension as was possible.

17

The Test

Ganesh-*pant* and his wife had a huge argument after Moro-*bhatta* left and poor Yamuna felt very guilty about it. But what could she do, given the unfolding drama in the household! She could only wait for the right moment! The next evening, Moro-*bhatji* arrived as promised to meet Ganesh-*pant*, bringing Deshmukh along. After the initial greetings were over, Moro-*bhatji* plunged right into the heart of the matter saying to Deshmukh: '*Rao-ji* here has suffered a terrible loss in his family. His only son has passed away. What rules and rituals do you advise for him in this context? We need to act urgently; swiftness is the need of the hour.'

Deshmukh: 'I am very sorry for your loss; I heard about it in Pune. Vinayak-*rao* was a really fine young man.'

Moro-*bhatta*: 'Fine people leave behind fine

legacies! Whatever one does, it is important to be mindful about one's reputation in society. After a person's death, no one should besmirch his name. No one should be allowed to do so! While *yajman* here completed all the death rituals and donated adequately—cows to Brahmins on the twelfth day of funeral rituals—there is still the lingering problem of the deceased's wife. Once a solution for that is found, there will be no place left for any criticism. We have consulted you on this, as you are a Brahmin of great status with a tremendous reputation and have prominent personalities among your relatives.'

Deshmukh to Ganesh-*pant*: 'It is obvious that criticism will automatically cease after the rituals are correctly followed, and in a timely manner. So, what remains now? You are Brahmins living in a prominent priestly, pilgrimage town. Your lifestyle and reputation are unblemished and you need to see to it that this standard is maintained. You must finish all your ritual commitments.'

Moro-*bhatta*: 'If we delay with the death and widowhood rituals any further, *yajman* will also be unable to invite Sri Shankaracharya to his home when the latter visits in the month of *sravan*. It is best to be done with the rituals.'

Deshmukh: 'Yes, our discussion here should be enough to convince *Rao-ji*! A sensible person, they say,

The Test

does not need to be explained the same thing twice.'

Saying this, they both immediately decided to go ahead with Yamuna-*bai*'s tonsuring at the river. Poor Ganesh-*pant* just sat there stupefied, listening to them deciding the details of his own daughter-in-law's tonsuring, as if he were in a daze. Meanwhile, Moro-*bhatta*, vindicated by Deshmukh's opinion went inside the house to explain the decision to Yamuna's mother-in-law. They decided to accomplish the tonsuring on the following day itself since it was the month-anniversary of Vinayak's death. Moro-*bhatta* promised to arrive at dawn the next day and take Yamuna with him to the river in a covered cart.

Ganesh-*pant* angrily muttered to himself: 'What kind of oppressive compulsion is this? Did I even say yes to this ritual? Without taking my consent and permission, how did these two simply decide to enforce the ritual on my family, bringing utter calamity on that poor and unsuspecting, innocent child? A meaningless fight would have immediately broken out if I had openly objected then and there, and the matter would have spread among my gossiping relatives looking for the slightest opportunity to come pecking at me like crows. The only thing I can do now, is to go away somewhere else for a few days. Let them do whatever they want behind my back! At least, I won't be there to see it. I don't have to incur the sin of breaking my promise to my son.' Thinking this, Ganesh-*pant*, full of the greatest disgust, left home that evening to stay for a few days at a distant farmhouse he owned.

The next day, Moro-*bhatji* arrived as promised, to take Yamuna to the riverside and though her mother-in-law tried to cajole her into coming out of her room, Yamuna refused. Then her mother-in-law began abusing and threatening her; but still Yamuna refused to come out of her room. Yamuna's mother-in-law was then forced to tell Moro-*bhatta* to return another day. Out of rage she locked Yamuna inside the room and did not give her food or water the whole day. Shivram and his mother, who were staying in the same house grew upset and distressed at this and began crying. Though Shivram had earlier been an undisciplined and stubborn boy, his nature had greatly transformed under Vinayak-*rao* and Yamuna-*bai*'s gentle influence. Though he had not begun reading or writing as yet, or going to school, he had great native intelligence. Of late, he had come to understand many things and had become thoughtful and introspective. His mother was uneducated, but she too had become attracted to the same religion that Yamuna-*bai* internally followed—the honest and straightforward path.

Shivram and his mother had stayed hungry the

entire day out of solidarity with Yamuna-*bai*. At night, Yamuna-*bai*'s mother-in-law dragged her out of the room by her hair and thrashed her black and blue with a broomstick. Then she dragged her outside the house to the backyard. Seeing this, Shivram and his mother rushed to Yamuna-*bai*'s aid and the four of them began struggling and tussling in the dark. Finally, Yamuna-*bai*'s mother-in-law let go and extricating herself, went back inside and banged the door shut. It was pitch dark and late at night as the three—Yamuna-*bai*, Shivram, and his mother—found themselves alone in the darkness, thrown out of home at an unearthly hour. None of them had eaten or drunk anything the whole day. Moreover, the violent, physical scuffle that had just taken place had exhausted them.

Yamuna-*bai* said to Shivram's mother: '*Bai*, you have been forced into this suffering only because of me. I am very sorry!'

Shivram's mother: 'What is there to feel sorry about? It was I who found your suffering unbearable! I have no one else, and I am not beholden to anyone else either. My son and I can walk away to another place whenever we want. But we remained here for your sake because we care for you and feel worried for you. Yours is a different case than ours.'

Shivram: 'But *aai*, why should *tai* (for elder sister

is what he had begun to affectionately call Yamuna-*bai* of late) continue to live over here?'

Shivram's mother: 'Where else will she go? Her father's household is no longer in town because he works abroad. Her mother is also long dead. Where will she go?'

Shivram: '*Mama* (for uncle is also what he had affectionately begun calling Vinayak-*rao* too) has a good friend in town. Why don't we go to his house? He will definitely shelter us. I know him well, and he had even sent *tai* a condolence letter after *mama* passed away. I know where he stays. Let us go there.'

While the mother and son were thus talking, Yamuna-*bai* was praying silently and trying to remember scripture verses that were meant to calm the sorrowful heart. The moment she heard Shivram say her husband's friend's name, she recognized it from the condolence letter he had written her.

She asked Shivram: 'Do you know where his house is? It is true that he wrote to me some time back, but I never found the time to reply.'

Shivram: 'Yes, *tai*, he is a fine gentleman. Let us go to him.'

Yamuna-*bai* thought to herself: 'Maybe this is God's hand. He is giving me the opportunity that I need to go forward on my path. There is no doubt that my moment of freedom is now at hand! It is time for me to leave, for if I continue staying here, I will be ruined. I give my life into God's hands.'

Then, after a short silence, she said to Shivram's mother: '*Bai*, I have made the decision to go to my husband's friend's house. Not to protect my body from pain; I leave this house now to protect my soul from destruction. If you both come with me, this will be a new path for you, too.'

Hearing this, Shivram cajoled his mother to accept Yamuna-*bai*'s decision and accompany her. Then, they all got up from the ground—for they had collapsed briefly after the tussle—and started walking. Shivram ran ahead to show them the path in the night's darkness. It took them a long time to reach their destination. It was almost eight in the evening by the time Shivram was knocking at Vinayak-*rao*'s friend's door. Daji-*ba*—for that was his name—immediately opened the door and came out on the veranda to welcome them. Shivram explained all that had transpired and the two women were immediately ushered in. Daji-*ba* was very pleased to meet Yamuna-*bai* and immediately said a prayer in gratitude for their arrival at safe harbours. He instructed his wife Lakshmi-*bai* to cook and care for the two women and the boy and they all sat together and prayed before eating. Yamuna-*bai* and her companions were so exhausted that they fell asleep immediately afterwards.

The news spread like wildfire the next day. Two Brahmin widows and a small boy had taken refuge with a Christian convert in town. Ganesh-*pant* too, came to know of it. He came forthwith to Daji-*ba*'s house, to meet his daughter-in-law. After patiently hearing her story, he said he was relieved that she had escaped the calamity looming over her. Despite the criticism going around, he decided to support Yamuna-*bai*. Those who criticized Yamuna-*bai* were in any case uneducated. He brought back all her clothes, belongings, and books from the house and though other Brahmins in town reviled Yamuna, Ganesh-*pant* continued to shower her with affectionate blessings. Daji-*ba* was a native Christian convert and preacher, and his wife Lakshmi-*bai* too, was a devout and pure-hearted convert. They were both kind-hearted and had a son and daughter.

Shivram knew them already, but staying together now strengthened their bonds. Shivram's mother became deeply influenced by Christianity, her new knowledge destroying all the remaining darkness in her heart. Her heart was now filled with the sunlight of truth. For those readers who may feel surprised about Shivram's mother's and Ganesh-*pant*'s seemingly quick change of heart, it must be said that Shivram's mother had already broken caste strictures, though in immoral ways. Ganesh-*pant*, on the other hand, had been inspired by natural, parental love for his youthful and innocent daughter-in-law. One can see thus, how God brings about good from the evil deeds of humans. Shivram's mother repented her sins, begged God for forgiveness, and learned how Jesus Christ had sacrificed himself to rid all humanity of sin. Through this realization, she could finally begin to see her own path forward towards salvation. Knowing this filled Yamuna-*bai* with enormous joy.

18

Shivram

The time has come for us to end this story and for our readers to finally know what the future held for Yamuna, Shivram, and his mother as the seeds of divine scripture sown in their hearts came to fruition. At first, as with plants, the sowing of seeds was followed by sprouts peeping from the earth, which then became strong enough to bear flowers. The flowers dispersed further seeds and gradually became transformed into fruit. Plants at a sensitive stage require additional care and providing this additional care is an arduous task. Similarly, as with religion, the imbibing of divine virtues had taken root in the hearts of Yamuna-*bai*, and for the mother-child duo—Shivram and his mother—their faith had slowly proliferated and strengthened. Yamuna-*bai*'s grief diminished gradually, as she found solace in religion. After some time, God introduced her to an educated and religious young man, who became a loving and caring husband to her. With time, Yamuna dedicated herself to her new life companion and the couple thereafter spent the rest of their years in happiness, helping others and praising God.

We take leave of our worthy readers now, after explaining Shivram's situation in more detail. Shivram, as our readers know, had spent his childhood in moral degradation. Born in Kashi, and accompanying his mother, he grew up in an environment of sin and immorality in Pandharpur. Like other undisciplined children of his ilk, he developed bad habits. If God had not had mercy on him, he would never have met Vinayak-*rao* and his family. What would have awaited him in the future then is only a matter of conjecture. After being released from his trap, he went on to gain higher education in Mumbai and worked hard at his studies. His thoughts and opinions were transformed through his education and these changes were, more than ever, reflected in a lengthy letter that he wrote to his friends. This letter mirrors his utter concern for widows and their terrible condition in Hindu society. Reading a copy of this letter will inform our readers about Shivram's future life-goals.

Dear Friends,

I won't be staying in Mumbai for too long now. I am planning to return to you all and to my dear mother, who awaits me. I am grateful for your regular and kind inquiries about her and it makes me happy to say that my mother is at last, comfortable and happy. My eyes fill with tears every time I compare her present condition with our earlier, terrible state. If I had remained in that state, I cannot imagine the hell I would be in today! What did my own people care about me back then? I wandered around Pandharpur, tonsured and bare-bodied apart from my little loin cloth, and no one cared. I begged for food and money, and got half a penny or two. When people did not help, they told me all kinds of lies. Sometimes I pilfered and stole. Running around aimlessly like a wild calf, my life was meaningless. When I think of my mother's earlier condition, I am filled with horror, pity, and pain.

There are crores of widows like her in India, who spend their days drowned in the same ocean of sorrow. Whenever I think of them, my eyes overflow with tears. When will our people ever become aware of their social duty and responsibility? When will the sorrows of our widows ever penetrate their hearts and break their icy coldness? I was recently reading about African slaves in America and their inhumane condition. I must say, their suffering resonates with the suffering of our widowed women. My question is, should we, as the new generation of educated youth, passively watch this terrible, unfolding exploitation and torture? How will our country ever progress, if we allow our women to suffer in this way? Does our nation and society not need them? Why don't those, who call themselves reformers and who endorse progress, come forward and free our widows from their suffering? There are a great many educated, knowledgeable persons in Mumbai who regularly discuss widow-remarriage. But as of yet, none of them have taken the initiative and come forward to marry a widow. This is a matter of great shame.

I know the abject difficulties our widows face from personal experience, for these were also the difficulties faced by my mother and my elder sister. I witnessed how cruelly hard-hearted Brahminical practices function, to turn the hearts of other Hindu castes like the Sonar, Prabhu, and Shenoy to stone. Will they ever accept their mistakes? Even entertaining such hope seems useless! Whatever happens from now on needs to be initiated by our generation. There is no time to expect gradual change from the future. While there are bound to be oppositions and obstructions in our path of reform, these obstructions have to be staunchly and confidently faced and eliminated.

There have been many great social leaders in the world, who were equally persecuted by thoughtless and uneducated people. Not only were they criticized and harassed, they were imprisoned or in extreme cases, executed. Still, with their commitment, sweat, and blood, these leaders strengthened the foundations of society. Their subsequent generations lived in a brighter present and future and the fruits of their labour were enjoyed by millions. Don't we, as reformist leaders, possess the same power to change society and take it forward on a progressive path? Many will be happy to support and encourage our social reform. In fact, our powerful, most excellent government has made an important new law that can help us. This law has been positively reported and lauded in prominent newspapers and magazines as a pathbreaking intervention, and has been extolled by intellectuals and scholars from esteemed educational institutions. So, what obstructs us now? Not only will we find support from the educated but we will also receive support from our administrators and bureaucrats.

Most importantly, the supreme being who oversees our deeds with great satisfaction and blesses us, the sea of mercy himself, God almighty, will help us in our new task. Despite this, if those who are rich, elite, independent, and educated would rather prefer to do nothing and simply watch our widows burning on the pyre of torture and humiliation, their sins will be counted as the greatest in all time! Though I agree that those who marry widows will initially face harassment and persecution, this should not frighten them!

Those who have made up their minds to propagate widow-remarriage should, in fact, organize themselves and establish a society that holds regular conferences. Reformers should present their essays and opinions in such conferences and debate their views to convince listeners and include them within their activist ambit. But they should not stop there; for in my opinion, there is no urgent need to organize such societies anew, at least in places like Mumbai. Many such intellectual and reformist collectives already exist.

Now is instead the time when its members should come forward, take action, and collectively attack the foe. The agenda of this bold attack has to be carefully and courageously planned. Our main foot soldiers must be faithful and committed men of religion who will unflinchingly work towards their aim of reforming the condition of widows, taken as a religious task. They should be resourceful, ever seeking new means to overcome the obstacles in their path, and be prepared to bear the losses that treading such a path entails. These foot soldiers would advertise the aims and activities of the society among the general public and help to finance widow-remarriage, establishing new branches across cities in Western India like Pune, Satara, Ahmednagar, Belgaum, Khandesh (Nandurbar),

Nagpur, Aurangabad, Bhopal, Baroda, Ahmedabad, and Surat. Our foot soldiers should personally develop the widow-remarriage movement, with every step collaboratively taking them and the movement forward.

Such an endeavour obviously requires funding and everyone should donate as freely as possible. The rich and the poor should come together and collectively take an oath to support the movement by donating one tenth of their monthly income to the cause. Recently, when the British government raised money in India to financially sustain the families of those brave soldiers who had lost their lives fighting in the great war in Europe, didn't the poor contribute to this cause? The collected sum amounted to more than a lakh of rupees. Couldn't such monies be collected for our widows and their young and orphaned children too, to uplift them from a life submerged in sorrow and neglect? This money must of course, be carefully used.

The society should help guardians, who due to their poverty or fear of community members, are unable to get their widows remarried. The society must also help widows and their families with court cases when such cases are filed against them. Popular booklets in support of widow-remarriage and the widow-remarriage act itself, must be printed and freely distributed. Furthermore, hired social workers and volunteers must carefully investigate families, who are either prepared to remarry their widows or are torturing them and forcing them to undergo tonsure. Village women should help social workers in this task since village women have access to inside information and are better at communicating with families in their own respective villages, to understand their mentality. All this information must be reported to the leadership committee of the society.

If an organized, funded movement in favour of widow-remarriage can be instituted and mobilized in India, it is not hard to imagine that widow-remarriages would soon become common. It is important for members and workers therefore, convince others about the benefits of widow-remarriage and also demonstrate that the movement itself is not organized for anyone's personal benefit or individual profit. It is organized for the improvement of society and for the betterment of widows. There is no selfishness or avarice at work here. Similarly, upon encountering opposers, members and workers must remain polite and respectful. They must ensure that their opponents become convinced of the ensuing chaos that would result from an increasing number of young, unmarried widows.

The benefits of widow-remarriage to family and society and finally to the nation, must be patiently explained as what it is—a practice that generates peace, progress, and dignity for both men and women. While this work blessed by God should initially proceed on such lines, society members and workers must continue to brainstorm over ever newer techniques of mobilization and implementation. Once such a society begins functioning and gaining influence, many Englishmen would also donate, apart from helping in kind and providing voluntary services.

Native Christians too, would hardly hold back from wholeheartedly supporting and donating to the venture since native Christians are, after all, an equal part of Indian society. They love the country as much as any other Indian, if not more, as they want their country to progress. There would of course be those, who would express doubts about the membership—raising questions regarding who would want to join such an organization in the first place. But once the society is established, its aim and work advertised and freely disseminated, surely the secretary will start receiving many letters from women asking for help.

Though it will be a slow start, requiring first a year or six months to gain momentum, the task at hand would be similar to that of a gardener, who must initially work hard to water and tend his plants and protect them from infestation. It is through this initial period of hard work that his plants would blossom. As time passes, the plants, growing stronger, would bear fruit and flower in plenty. Similarly, if one continues to be patient, prayerful and asking God for blessings and guidance, focus on the task at hand and work hard, there is no doubt that our movement would reap a bountiful harvest.

I am well aware that thousands of young widows find no opportunity to express their desire of remarrying. Even if they want to remarry, they are afraid to speak out as they have no other place of refuge but with these same families that disallow widow-remarriage. They are forced to remain silent. According to the many letters I receive from friends and associates, these widows will certainly remarry, given the opportunity. If that be true, then why are we denying them their natural desire? Or pushing the decision into the future because we don't want to take its responsibility today? Or then, harbouring secret desires that force everyone to resort to immorality—this immorality specially plunging widows into additional humiliation and suffering?

Is it not evident enough from the various instances we hear of every day—of someone's widowed daughter having run away, or someone's widowed sister having become pregnant—that widows are, in fact, willing to remarry? If widows had not desired conjugal happiness, then why would they have engaged in immoral escapades? Instead of letting them sink into sin, isn't it better to allow them to respectfully remarry? Even if many widows are unwilling, out of the fear of stigma or embarrassment, aren't there many other widows who are sexually exploited, run away from home, and predictably resort to immorality? Why should we not provide for these women—giving them meaningful and respectable alternatives to rebuild their homes and families?

It is my wish to transcend the words I am writing today and transform these words into action. I would exhort reformists to initiate concrete action and join the government's popular endeavour for social emancipation. We must collectively establish the trailblazing society for the 'Propagation of Widow-remarriage' in western India, and in order to do so successfully, closely learn from western countries and emulate their functioning and the administration of other publicly funded societies and organizations. We should especially learn from England, Scotland, Ireland, and America that run large Christian organizations and missions across the globe.

Since these are charitable organizations dependent on public funding and hardly supported or answerable to the state or the crown of their country, these organizations function independently of the government, disseminating their agenda widely through public lectures that convince people of their intent while additionally inviting philanthropists and benefactors. In this way, over a period of time, they collect enough money to employ missionaries who travel far and wide, spreading information about the mission's goals. Their funds are used for running schools, churches, and social work activities. The lakhs of rupees that are annually collected are not donated by just one or two rich endowers either, but by ordinary people—even poor people donate as much as they can spare. Every penny collected is important since every penny contributes to the crores, collected over two or three years. So, why should we not emulate them?

The only caveat is that we will have to work hard; our society won't succeed if we remain passive. Our organizing committee members must focus entirely on proliferating the society's aims and making it successful—working with the same intensity as when working for personal benefit. This is the main reason for the enormous success of Christian missions today. Their annual transaction amounts to crores of rupees and they are so large that they function like government offices. Though I don't want to comment on Christian missions here, apart from reiterating that they receive abundant blessing from God, I only speak here of the power of human endeavour, prayer, and labour, and its propensity to succeed.

Finally, every human desires personal glory and we Indians are no exception in being especially thirsty for recognition. We expect our government to appoint us to important positions, pay us high salaries, accord us importance in newspapers and through meetings like the Bombay Association and promote us enough for our fame to reach Europe. But this glory is hardly real! Although there is nothing wrong with working in a government office and earning a salary and in fact, such positions do bring honour and authority to humble activities, real glory does not lie in amassing wealth or in gaining an education that is kept to oneself. Glory does not lie in building palatial homes and gardens and spending hand over fist in wedding ceremonies and religious rituals.

If tomorrow, a Hindu becomes the governor of Mumbai, it does not mean that he has achieved personal glory since logically speaking, not all the governors of Mumbai before him were great or glorious either! There are very few like Lord Elphinstone. To be a great person, one has to first serve society as a committed change-maker and reformer—like Luther, Columbus, Harvard, or Wilberforce. On the other hand, while it is impossible for every person to be glorious, it is important, in however humble a manner, to strive fearlessly and without discouragement towards one's goals. Indians should strive to reform their country and abolish widowhood practices that are cruel and dangerous. Widows should be treated exactly like widowers. Just as widowers remarry, widows should also remarry in a move that will provide men and women equality before God.

Reformers, who undertake this task as a personal endeavour and religious duty will be recognized in the times to come as the greatest of all global leaders. They will receive countless blessings from suffering and toiling young widows from across the country. So many girls will thank reformers for saving them the pathetic fate of being born to widows who were disallowed from remarrying! If not for reformers perhaps, these young girls would have already met their deaths in infancy, stifled and choked to death at some dirty street corner, their bodies thrown into public toilets and garbage heaps, their skulls cracked open, their faces, eyes, noses, and ears pecked by crows, and eaten by dogs. Even if they had escaped this cruel death, they would have ended up as prostitutes in brothels, their sons and brothers condemned as prostitutes' children and brothers. These boys would spend the rest of their stigmatized lives as alcoholics and addicts, begging and stealing for survival.

All of them would thank reformers, who through their enablement of widow-remarriage, would have enabled the rehabilitation of widows, helping them to return to a normal life and to respectable decency. Contemplating this cruel and horrible fate, now thankfully averted, all women and children facing it would bless reformers. The names of these reformers will be taken with gratitude and admiration throughout the forthcoming generations. So, dear friends, it is through such deeds that real glory and fame are achieved and if educated Indians were to chase this glory, our country and society would progress tremendously towards collective glory. It is useless to feel afraid of uneducated and thoughtless people in this journey since this fear will only serve to ruin the country and take it backwards. Instead, reformers of the younger generation should take the decisive step forward towards progress, treading in God's path with courage, tolerance, patience, and the acceptance of all the difficulties that lie ahead in their wake.

Glossary

Adityaloka: The realm of the Gods

Ba/Baba: Honorific title, an address for someone older

Bachcha: Child, an address for someone younger

Bai: An honorific title, an address for a respectable lady

Bhagawan: God

Bhakri: Unleavened bread made of millet

Bhakta: A devotee

Bhakti Marga: The path and method of devotion

Bhang: A powerful opiate made from a paste of marijuana leaves and buds

Bhat/Bhatji/Bhatta: Brahmin, an honorific address for a Brahmin priest

Brahmacharya: A period of studentship and celibacy practised by upper-caste men

Brahman Sabha: A conference of Brahmins that evaluates and prescribes the moral behaviour of the regional community

Chandrakala: A traditional saree spun in black cotton or silk and brocade, considered auspicious, and the special attire of married women on occasions such as Makar Sankranti

Chaturmasa: The four holy months that include *Shravan*

Dada: Elder brother, and an honorific address

Dakshina: Charitable fees offered to holy persons for their knowledge and blessings

Dharmashala: Hostels within pilgrimage towns where the poor can stay free of charge

Dhoti: Indian attire for men

Durva: Long stems of grass used in rituals

Dussehra: Festival of the autumn harvest marked by Goddess rituals

Ekadashi: The sacred, eleventh day of each lunar phase of a month

Grihasta Ashrama: A prescribed life stage of domesticity that encompasses marriage, children, and family

Inam: An imperial gift of land from which taxes could be used personally by beneficiaries

Janmasaubhagyavati: A prostitute, who can never be widowed, for having multiple paramours

Ji: An honorific vocative for men

Kanyadaan: The ritual gift of a daughter to the bridegroom in the marriage ceremony

Kasar: Caste of bangle makers and makers of beautifying products used by married women

Khandesh: North-western regions of Maharashtra, encompassing the Dhule, Nandurbar, and Jalgaon regions

Kirmiji: Crimson

Kirtan: Devotional songs

Glossary

Kumpini: The British East India Company

Kunbi: Caste of peasants

Mai: Mother, an honorific address for older women

Mali: Caste of gardeners

Mama: Maternal uncle, an honorific address for slightly older men

Mangalsutra: A special necklace worn by married women signifying their marital status

Maratha: Caste of landowners

Ovi/Ovya: Verse/verses

Panigrahan: The marriage ritual—the joining of the bride and bridegroom's hands

Pant: Brahmin householder, an honorific address for an elderly Brahmin householder

Peshwai: A period of 18th-century Maratha history that saw the proxy reign of the Konkani Chitpavan Brahmin prime-minister called Peshwa. A hereditary position, the *Peshwai* defines that period of the Maratha empire controlled by Konkani Chitpavan Brahmins

Pitrupaksha: A sixteen-day period in the lunar calendar for paying ritual homage to ancestors

Prabhu: Caste of Kayastha

Pradosh: The ritual point of transition between the bright and dark halves of the month

Prastavana: An introduction

Puja: Ritualized worship

Pustak: Book/volume

Rao: Landowner, an honorific vocative for a landed person, and the future inheritor of land

Rudraveena: An ancient stringed instrument used for playing Indian classical music

Saheb: A senior beyond personal access, an honorific address for a bureaucrat or official in a high government position

Saree: Indian attire for women

Shastri: A scholar of Sanskrit scriptures, an honorific address for someone who is knowledgeable

Shet/Shetji: Businessman, an honorific address for an affluent businessman

Shimpi: Caste of tailors

Shradhha/Varshik Shradhha: Funerary rituals carried out by family or descendants/annual funerary ritual carried out by family or descendants

Shravan: One of the holiest months (in August) of the Indian calendar that is part of the four months of *Chaturmasa*

Shudra: The lowest varna among the four: Brahmin, Kshatriya, Vaishya, and Shudra

Sonar: Caste of goldsmiths

Tai: Elder sister, honorific address for a slightly older woman

Tambat: Caste of copper braziers

Tulsi: Indian basil plant, considered a protective symbol of domesticity and worshipped by women in the family

Vaani: Caste of shopkeepers or grocers (followers of Shaivism called Lingayat in Maharashtra and Karnataka)

Vaidya: Traditional doctor